SIMPLE MANDALA COLORING BOOK

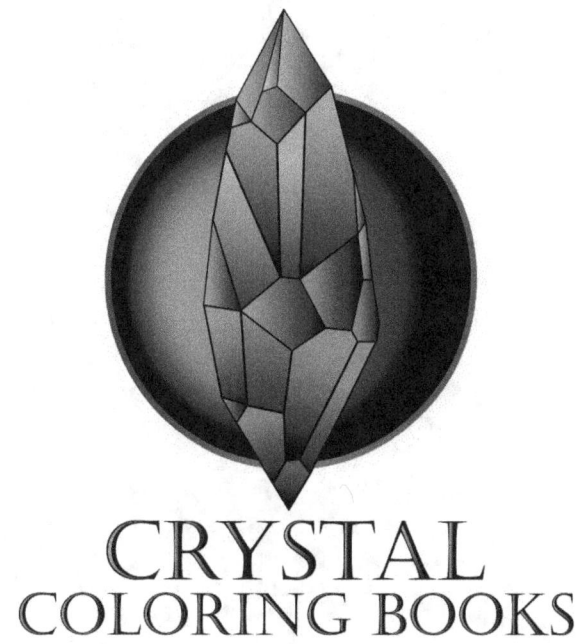

CRYSTAL
COLORING BOOKS

ISBN-13: 978-1983662621
ISBN-10: 1983662623

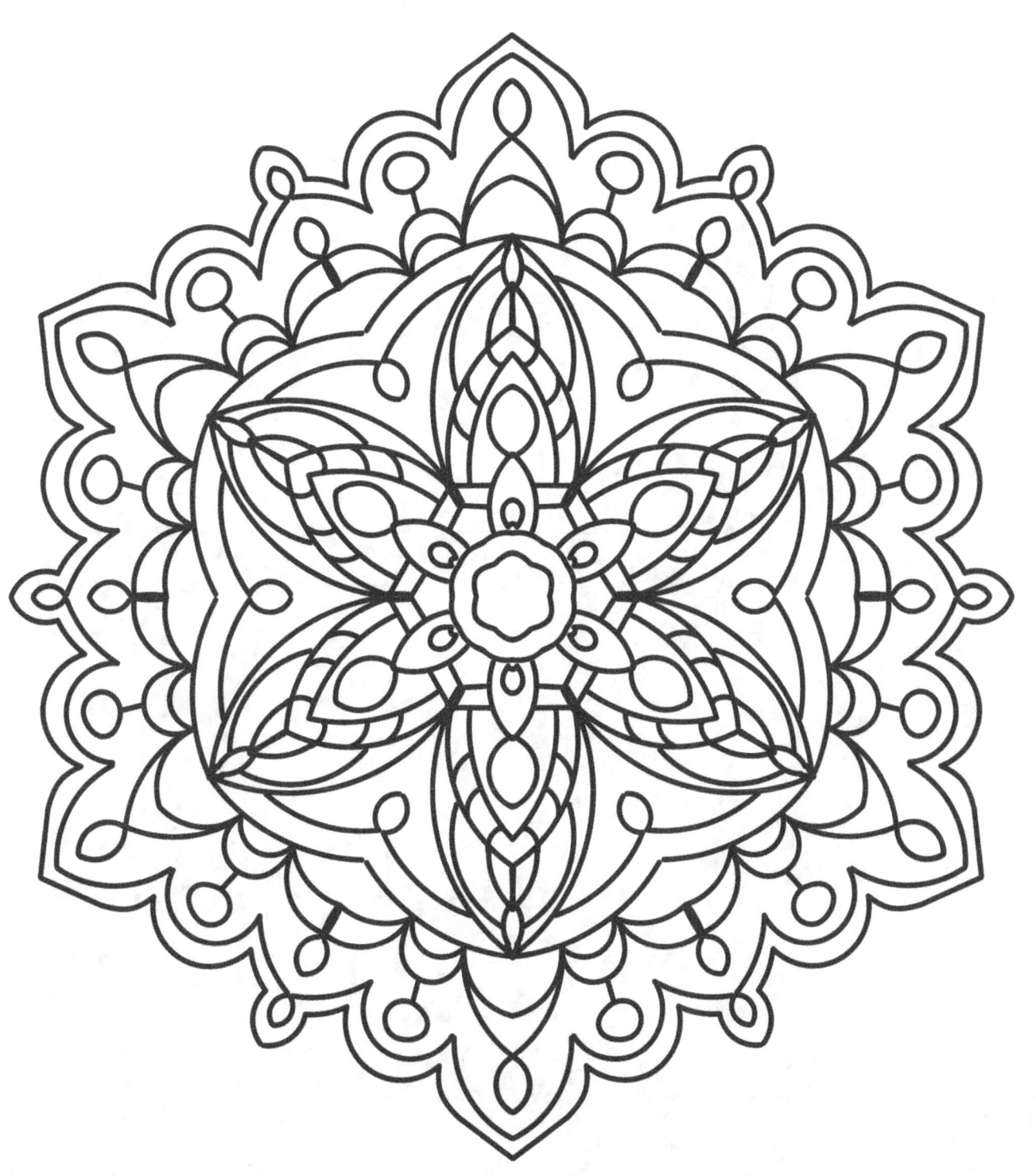

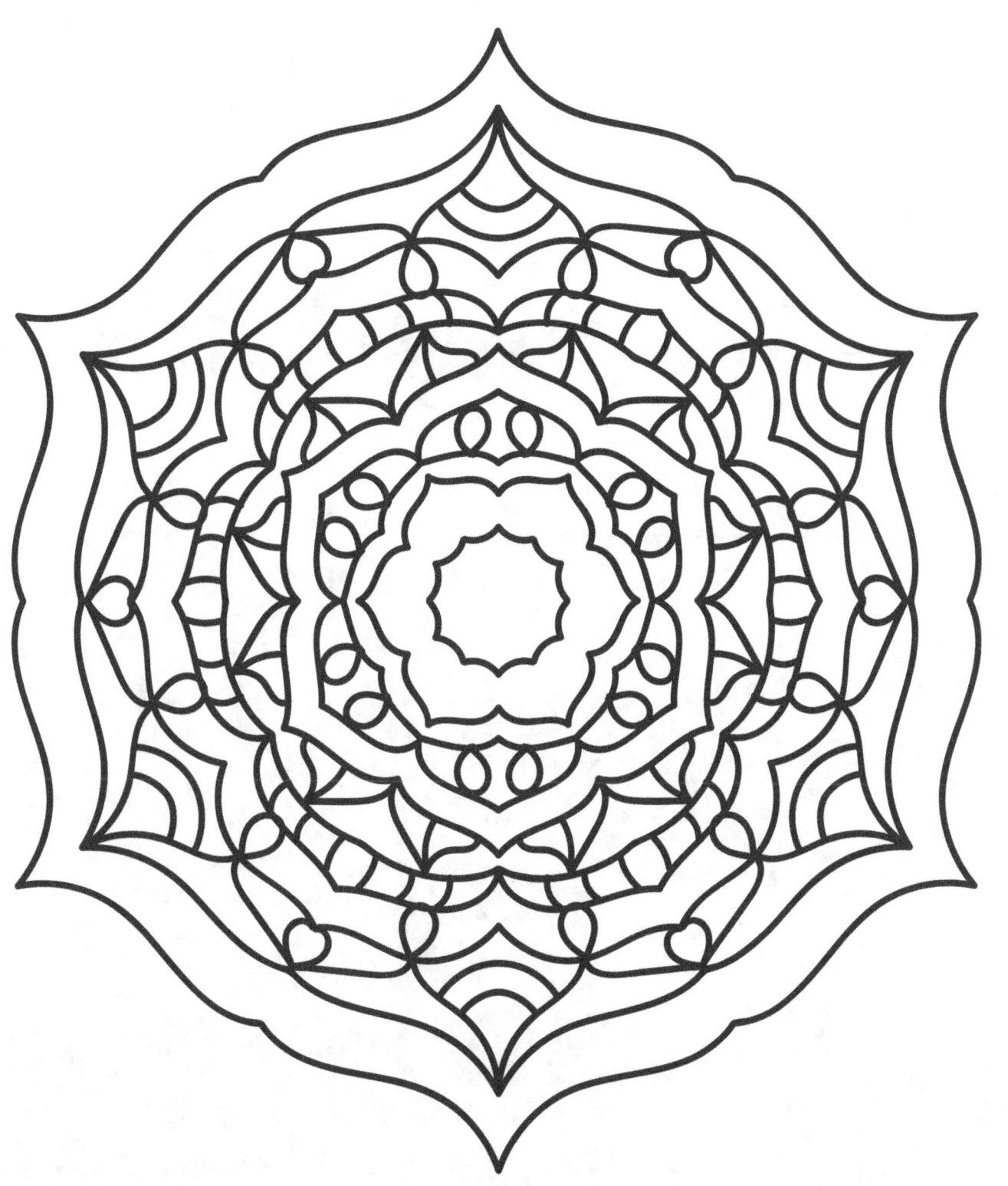

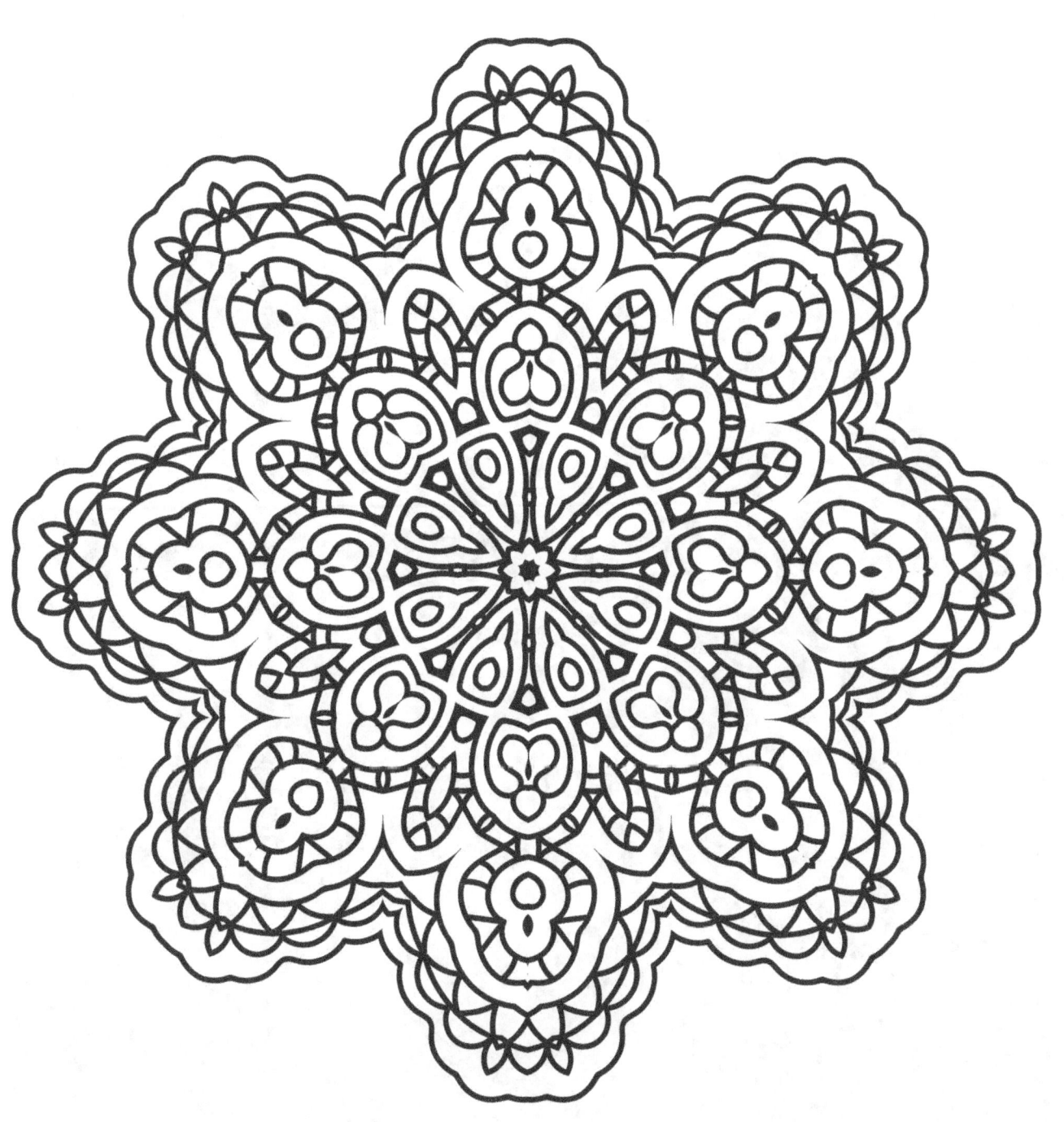

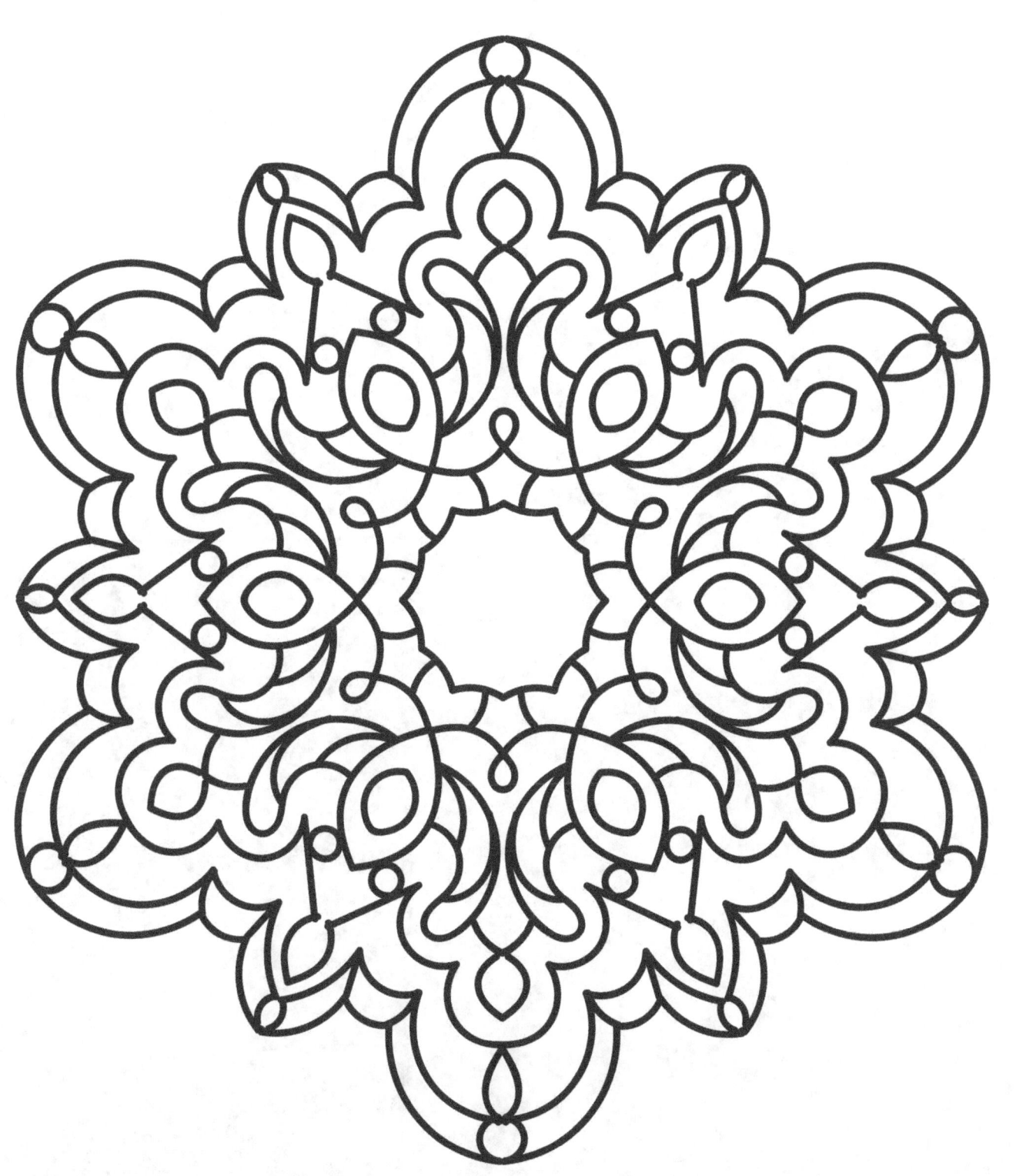

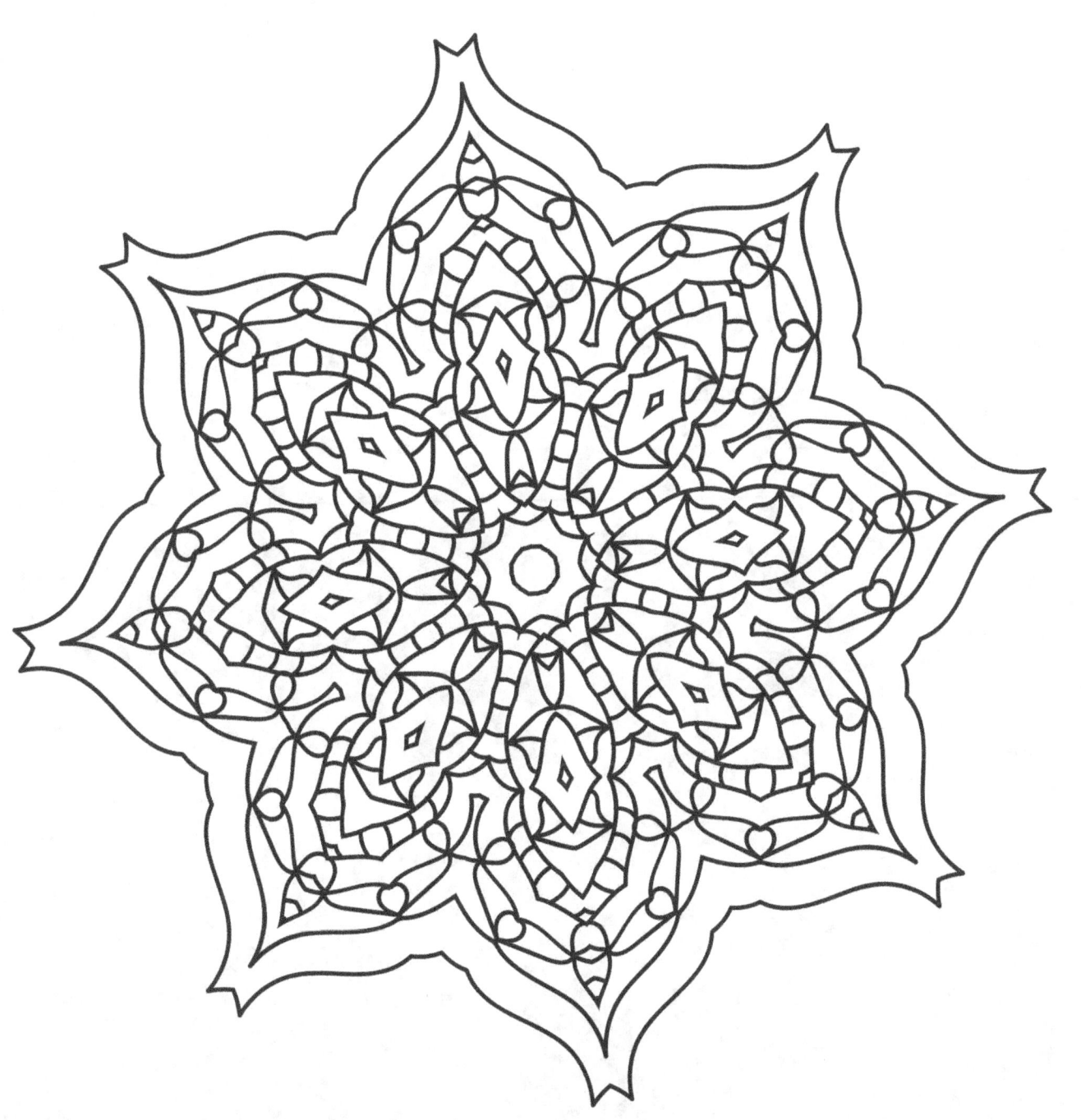

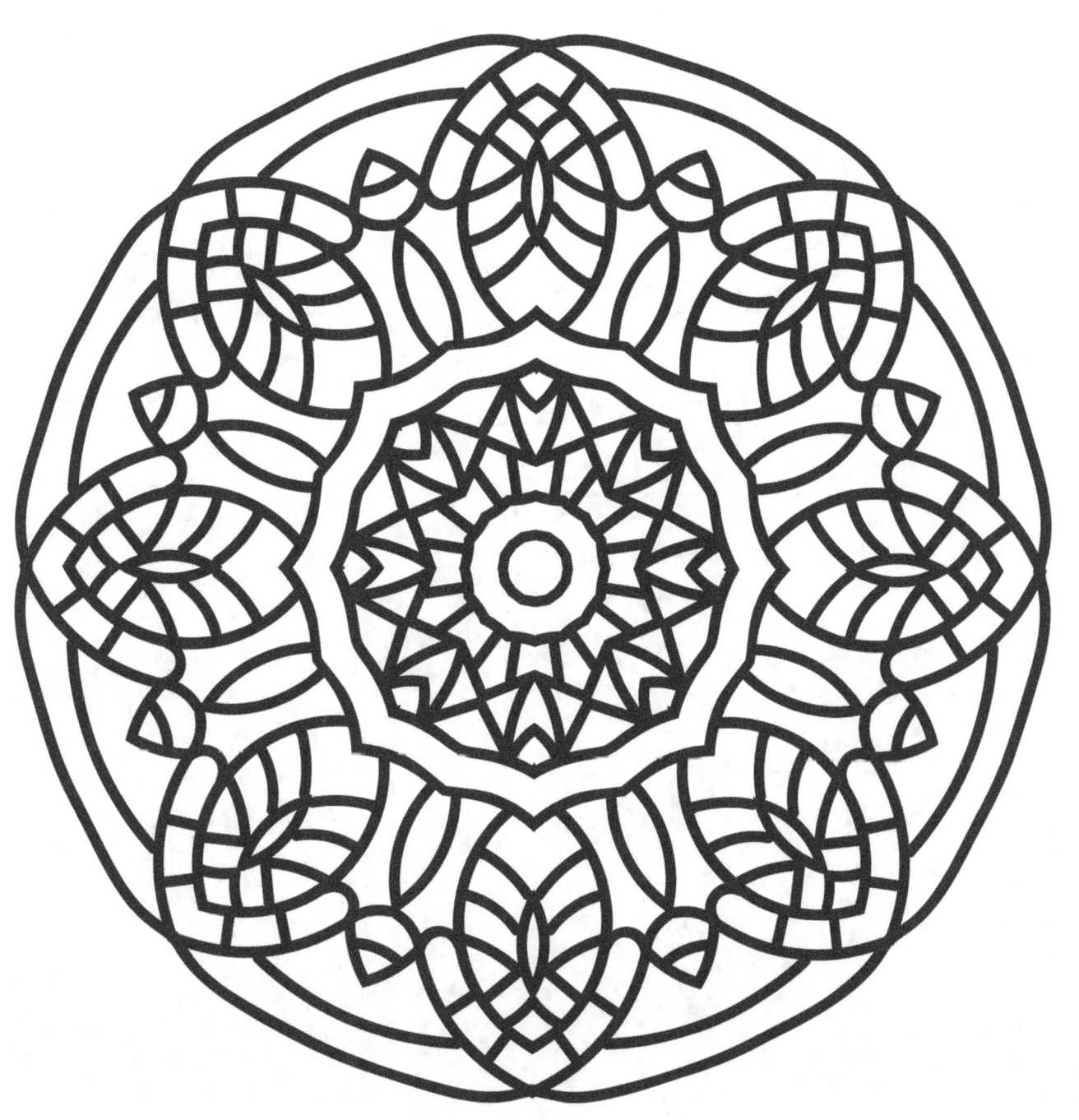

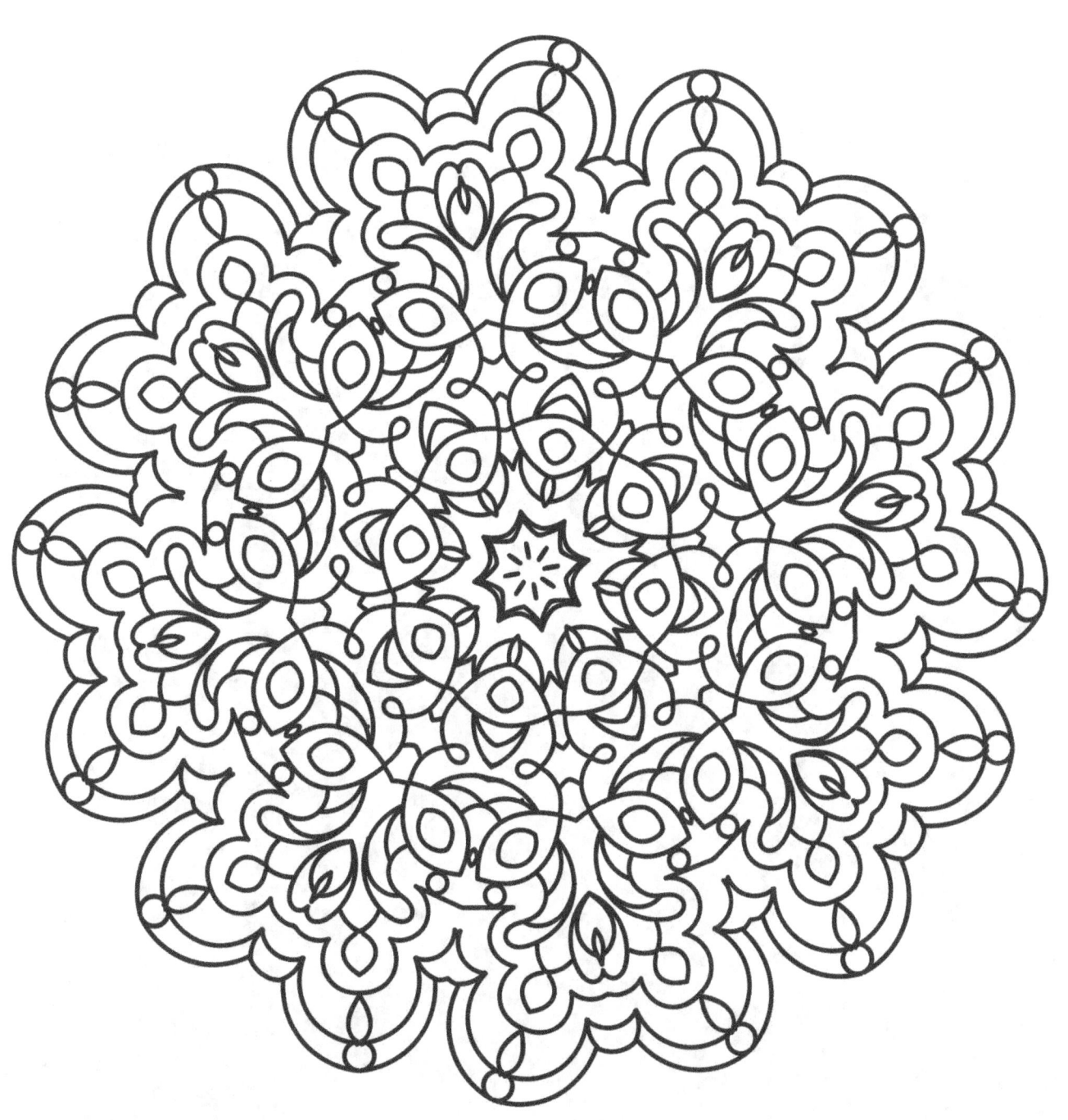

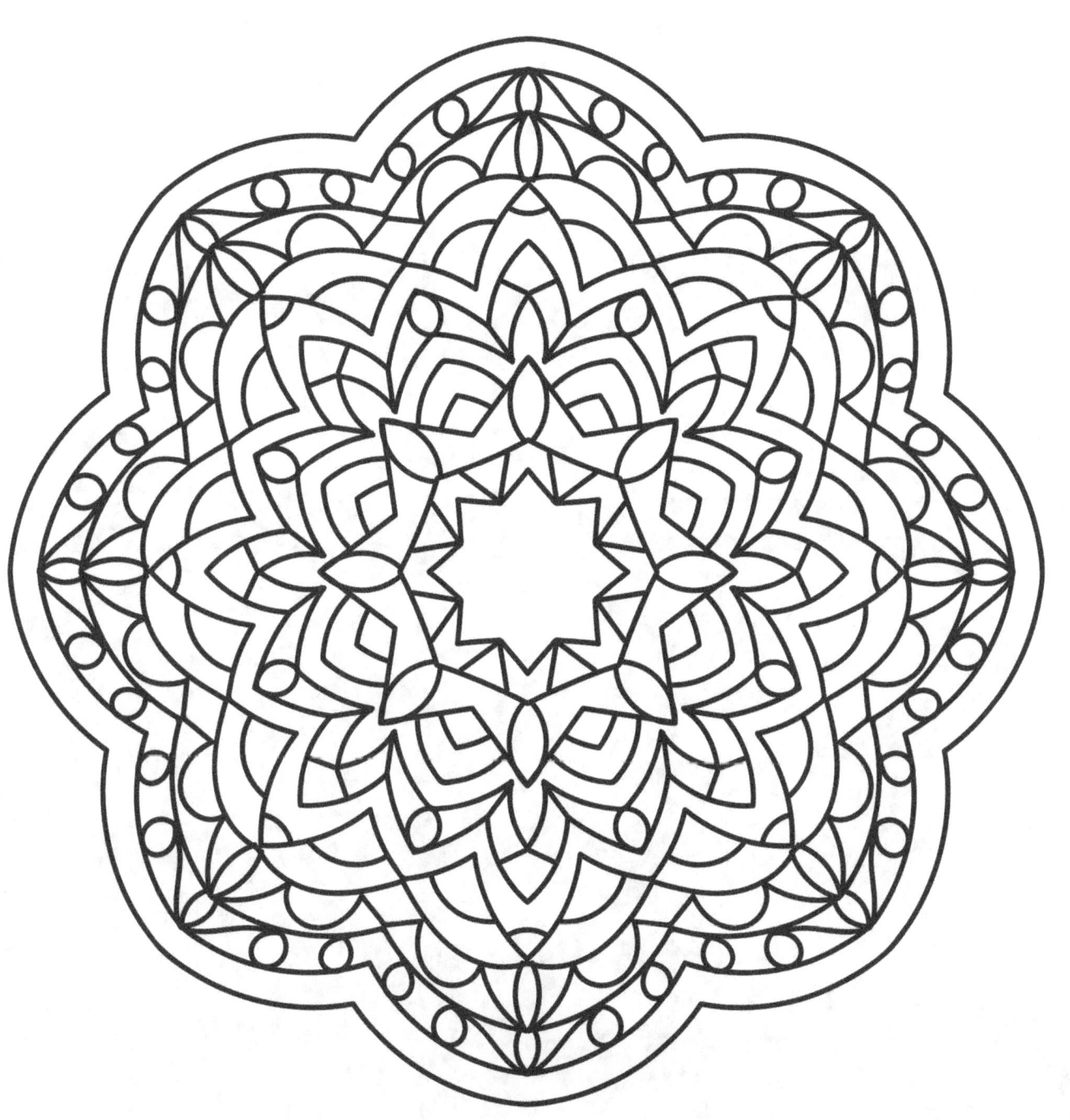

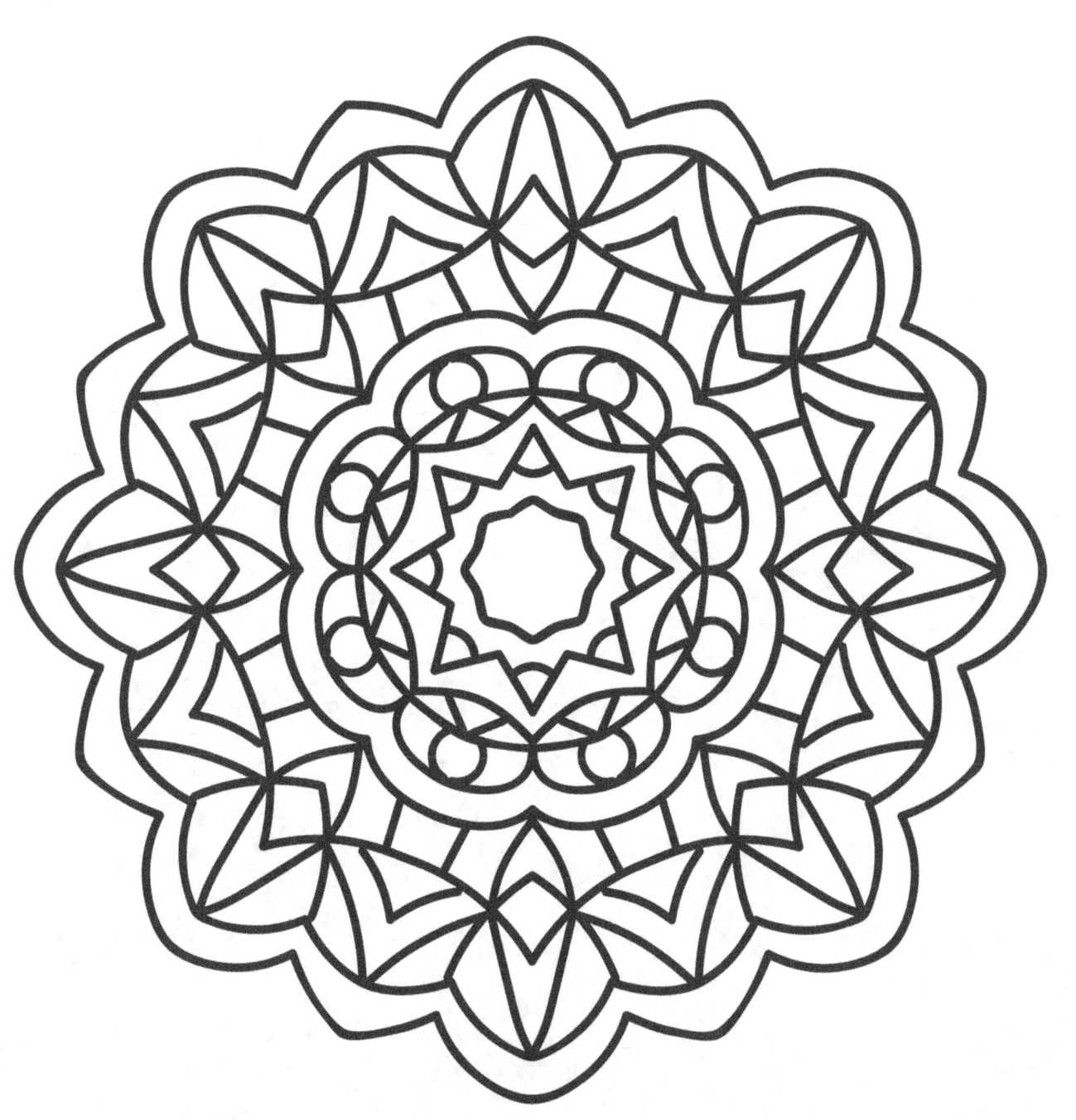

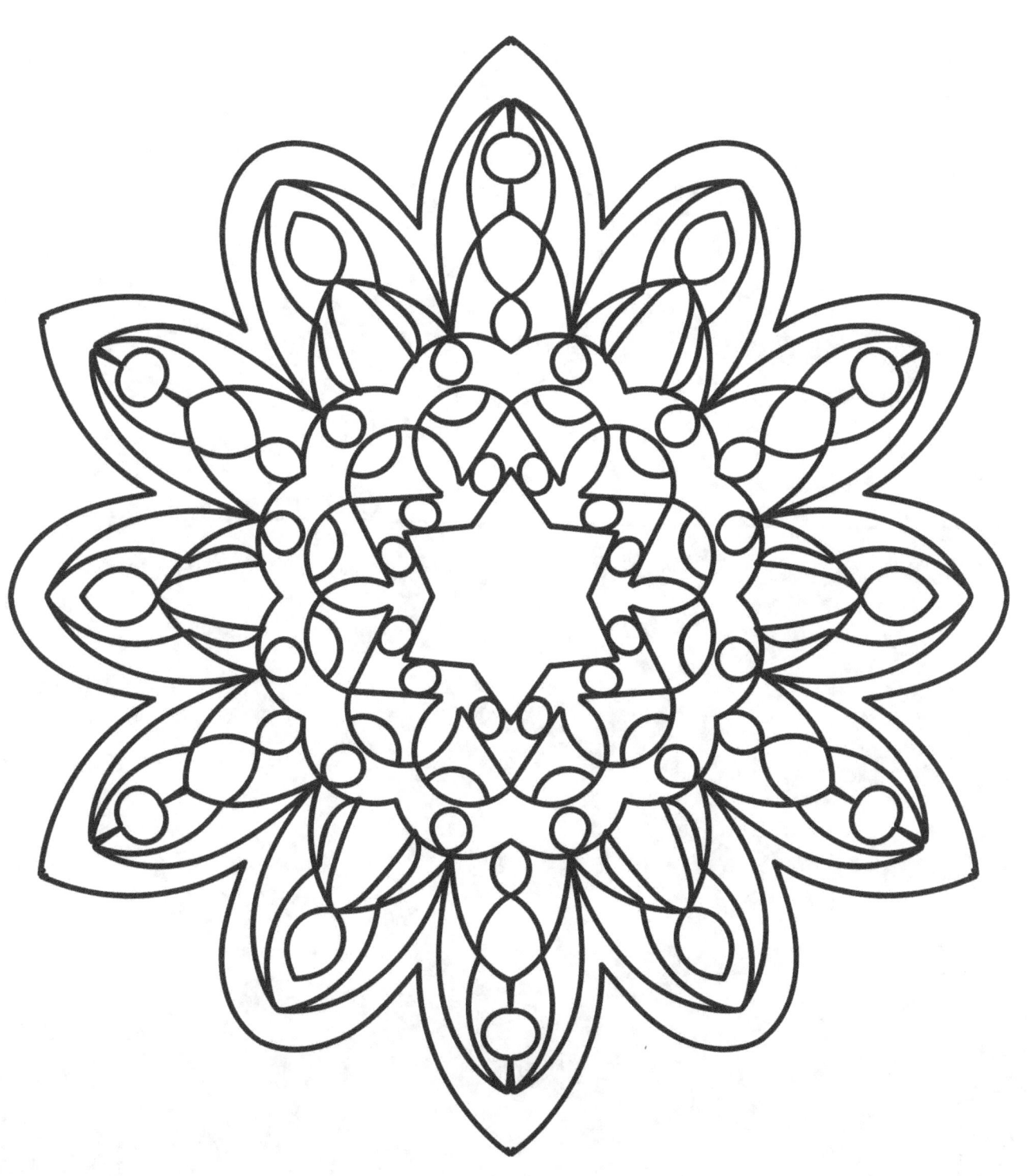

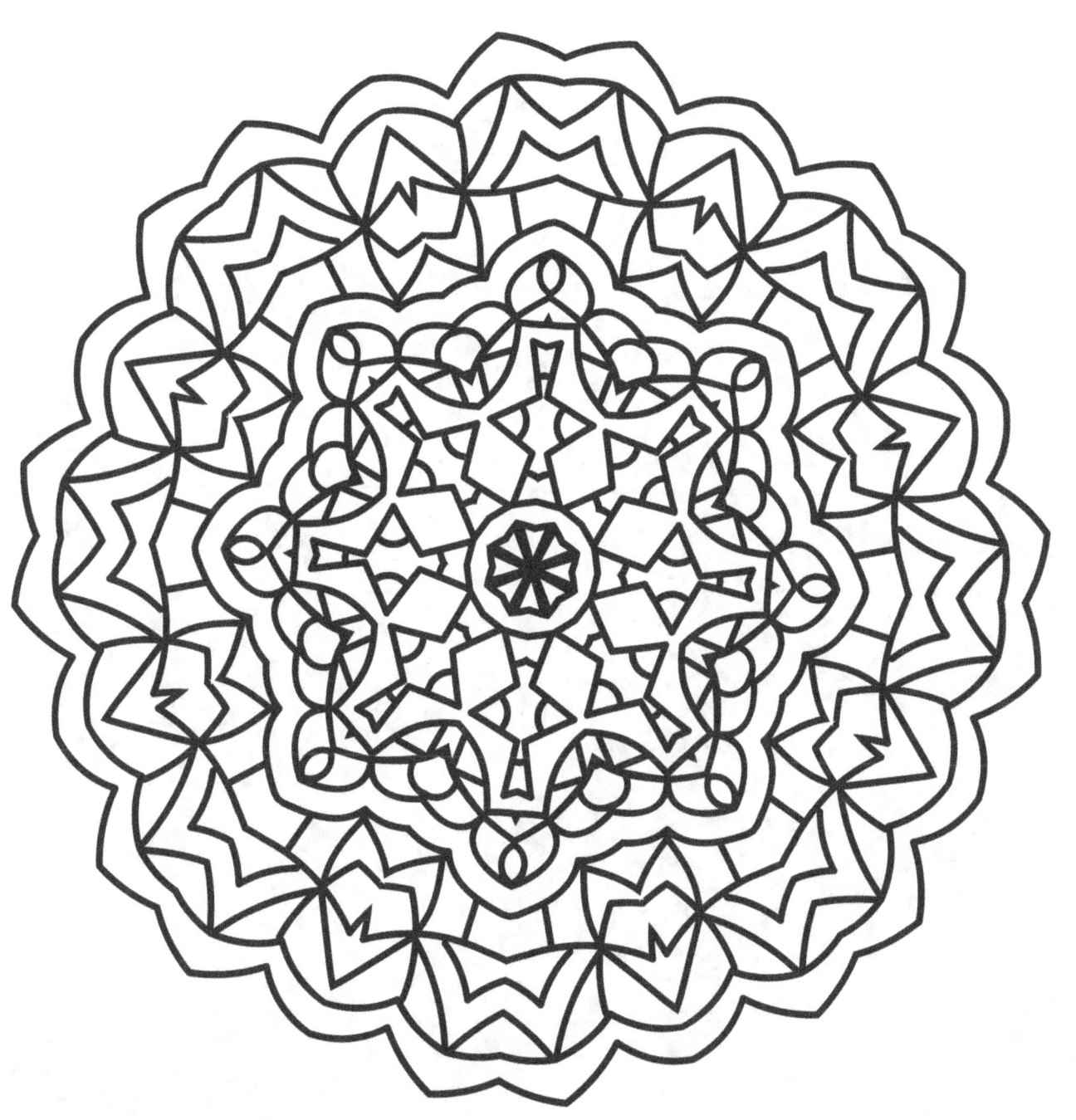

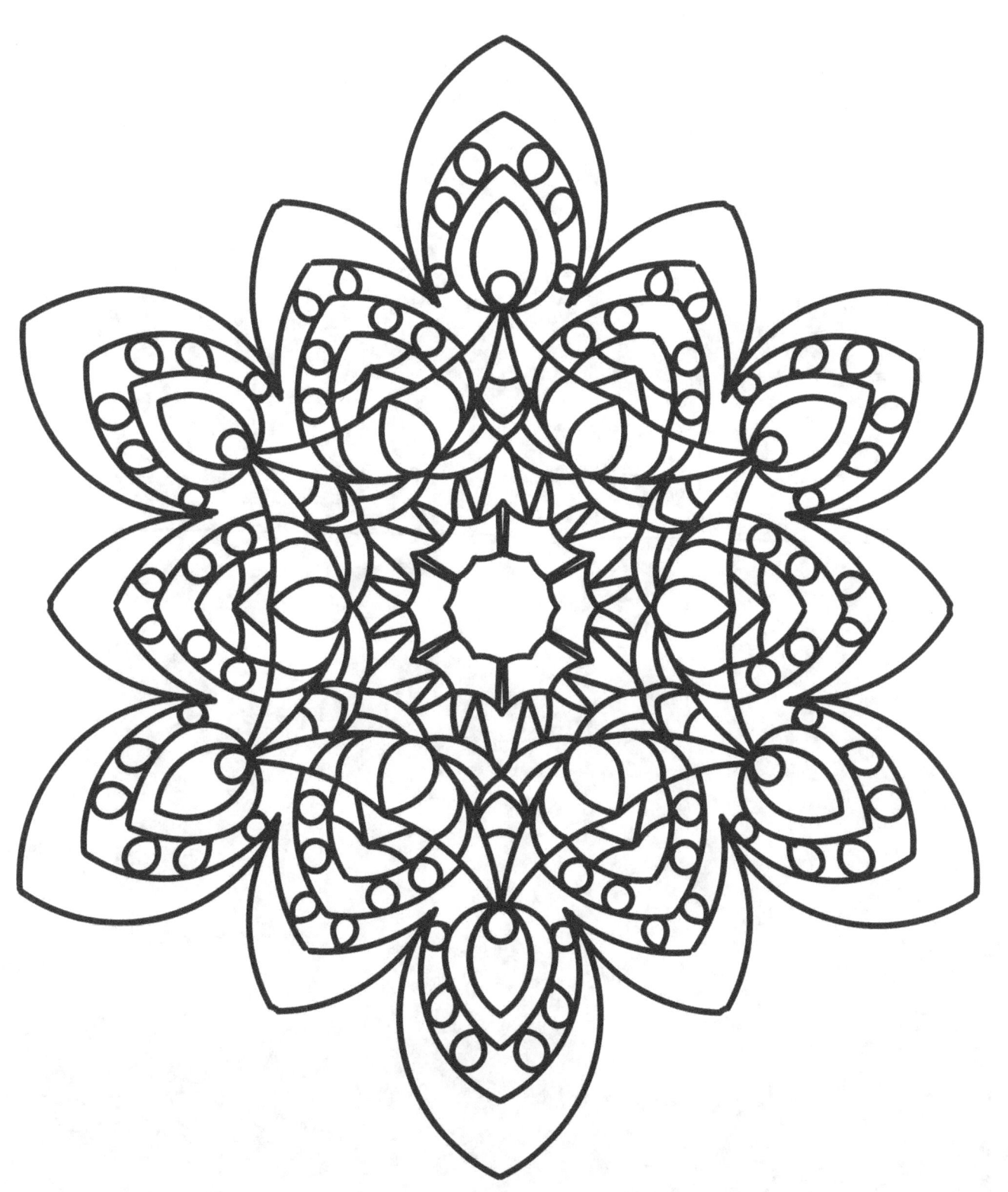

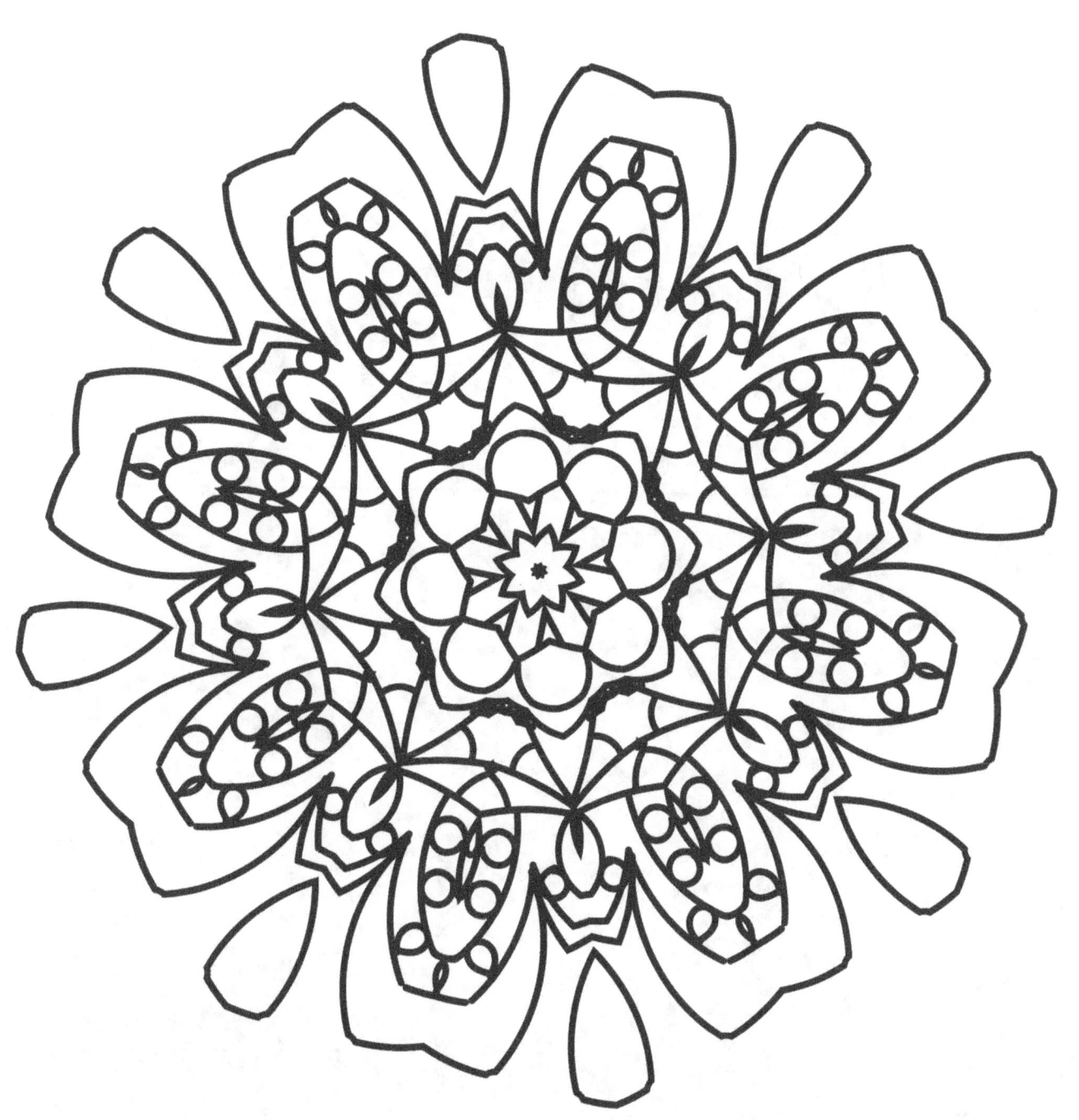

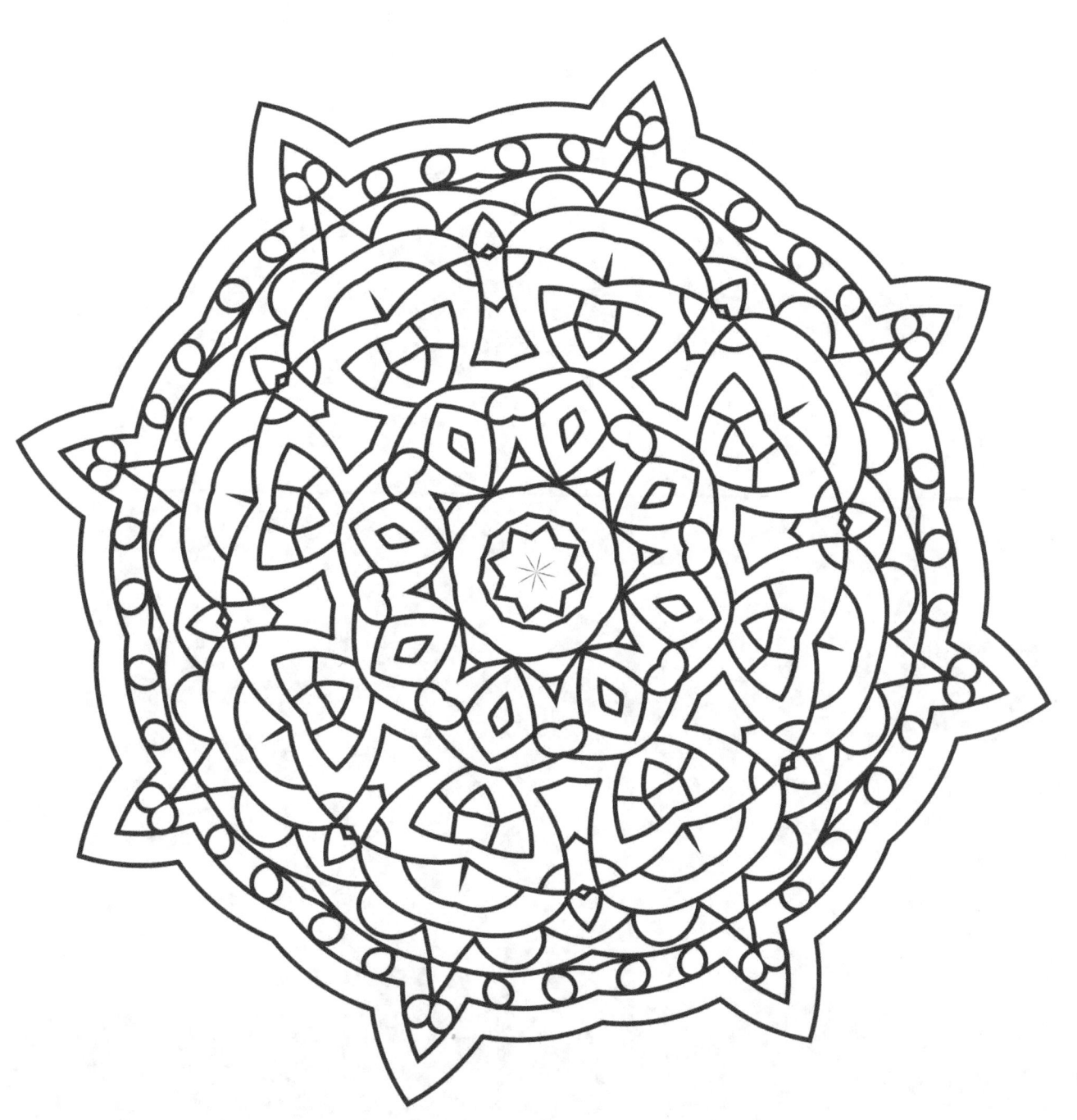

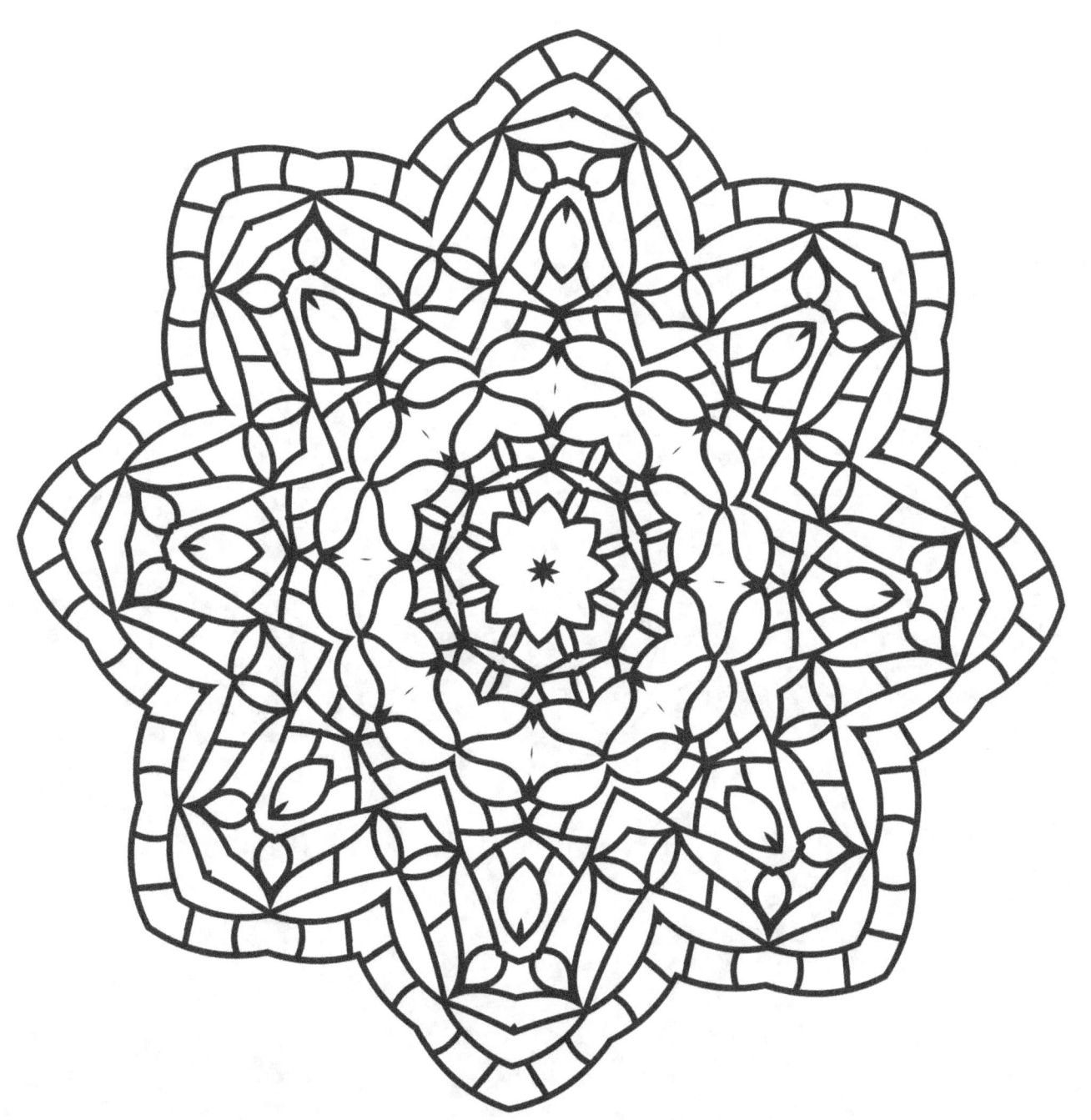

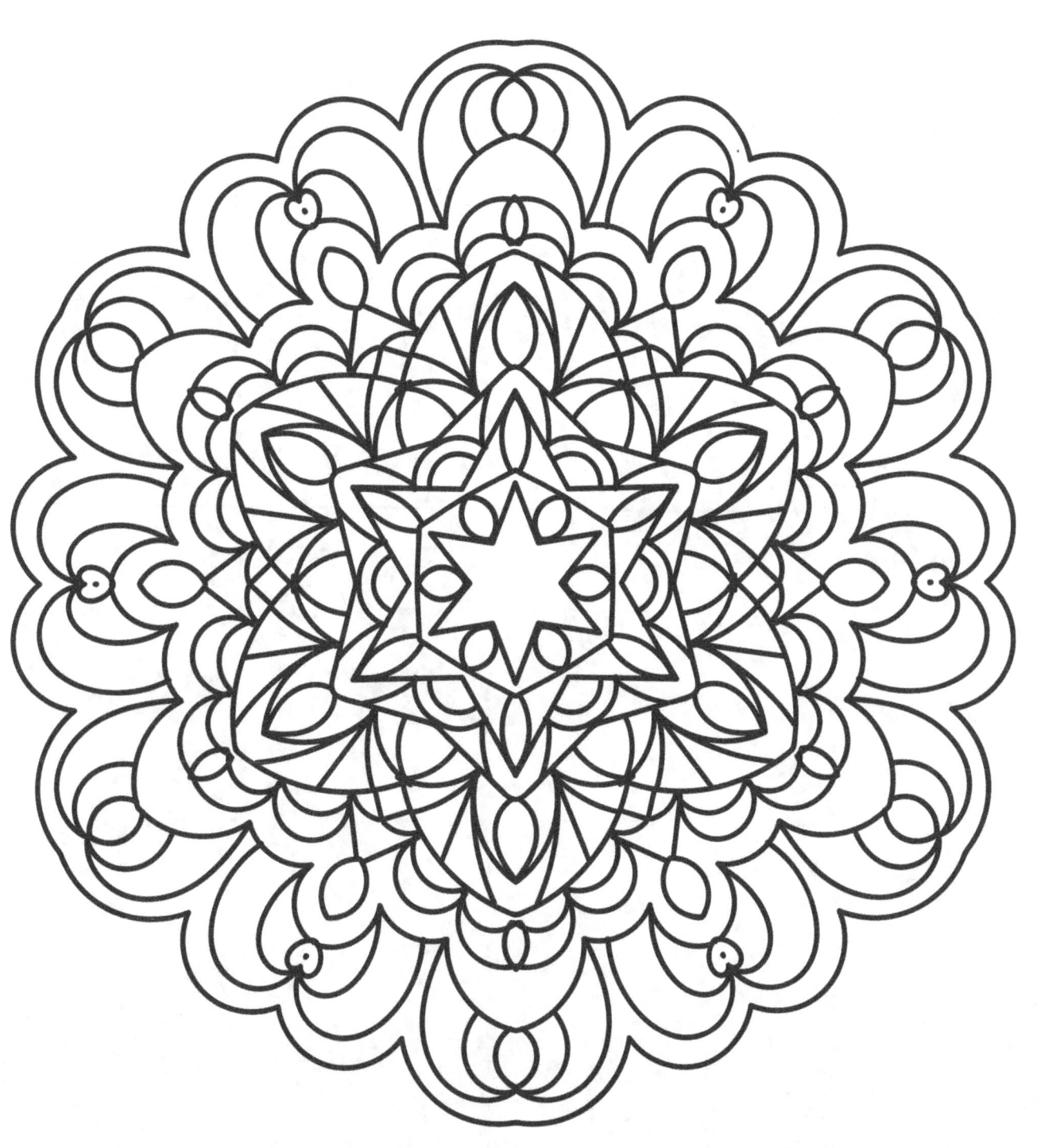

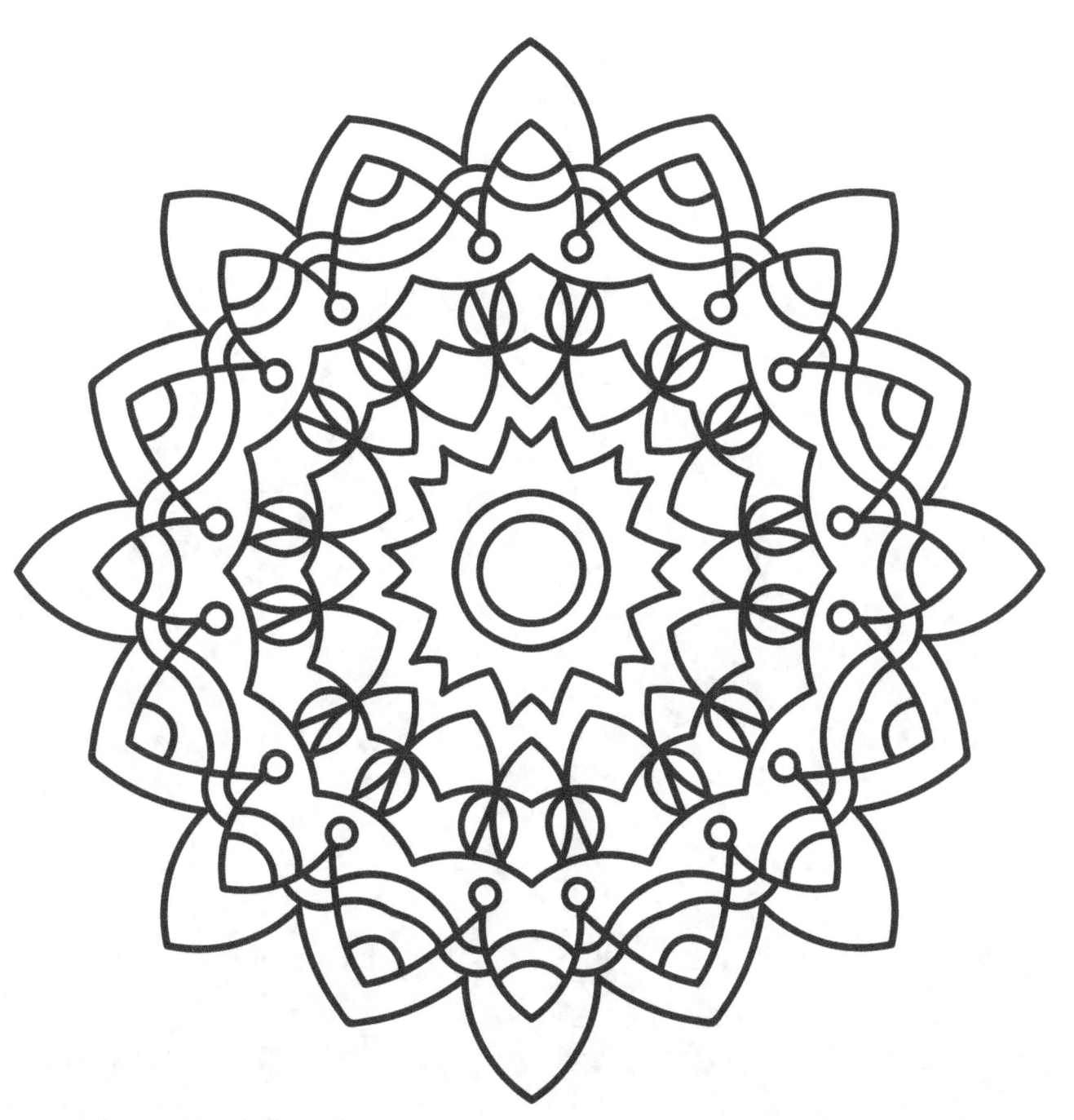

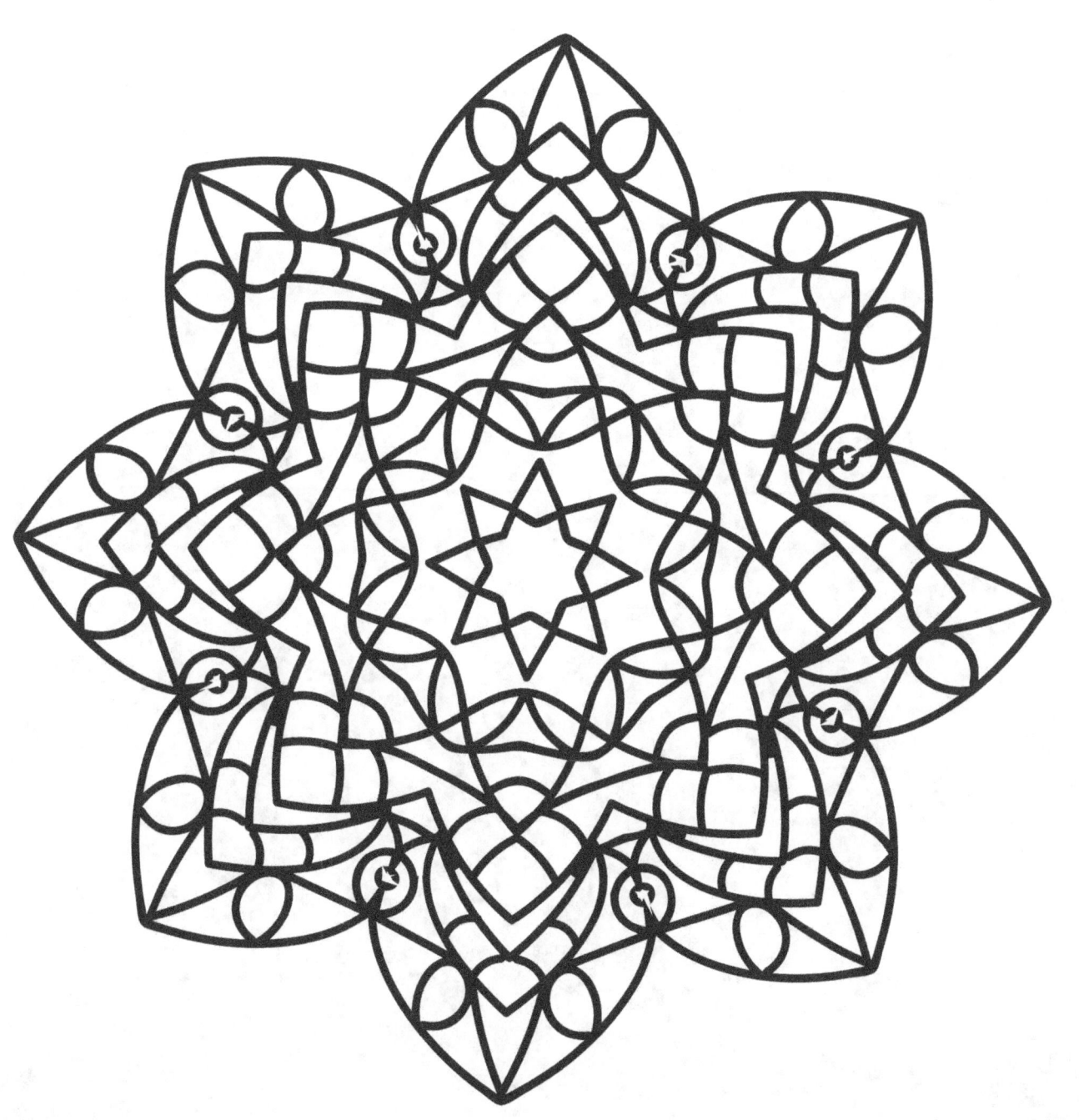

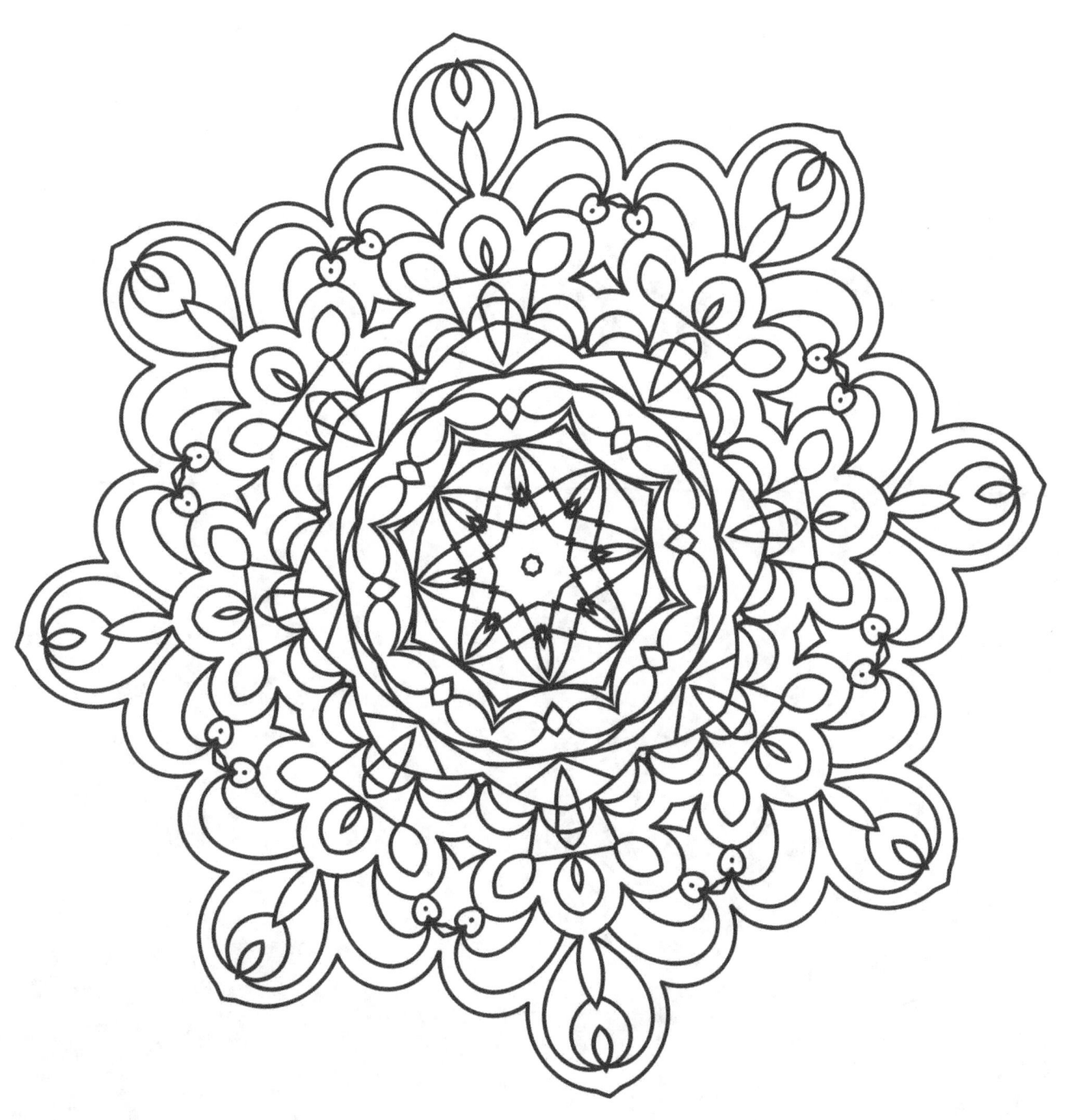

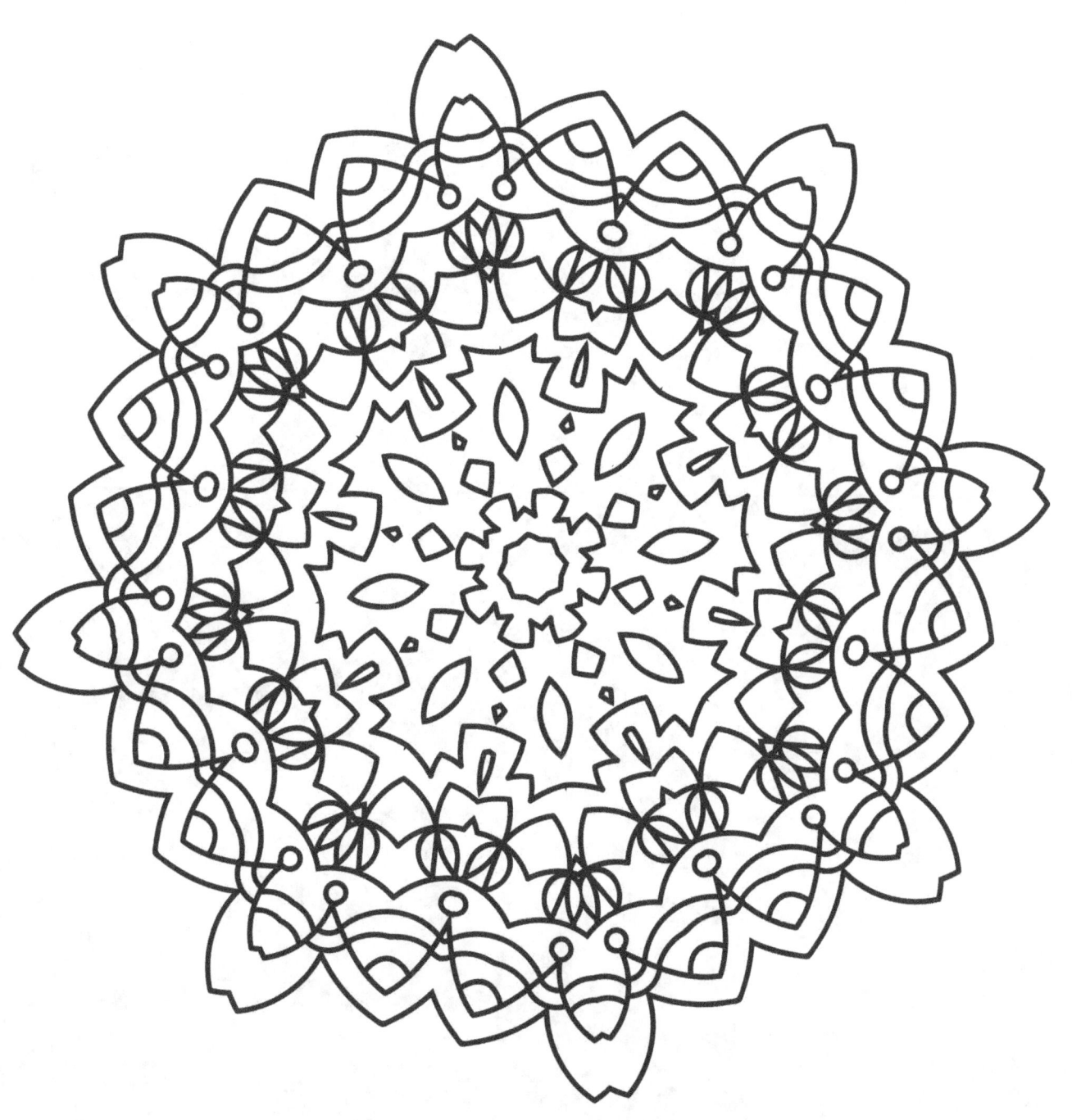

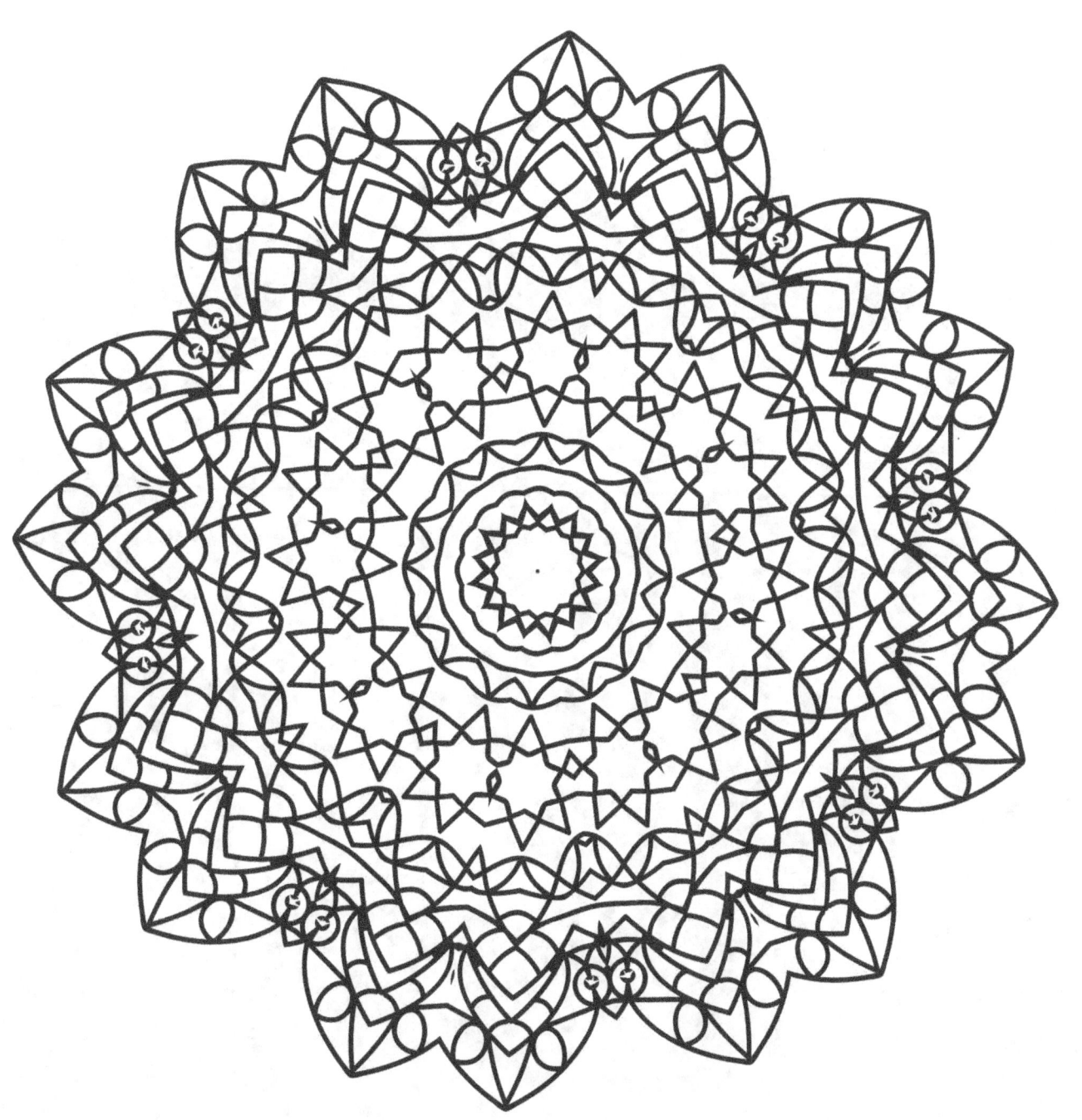

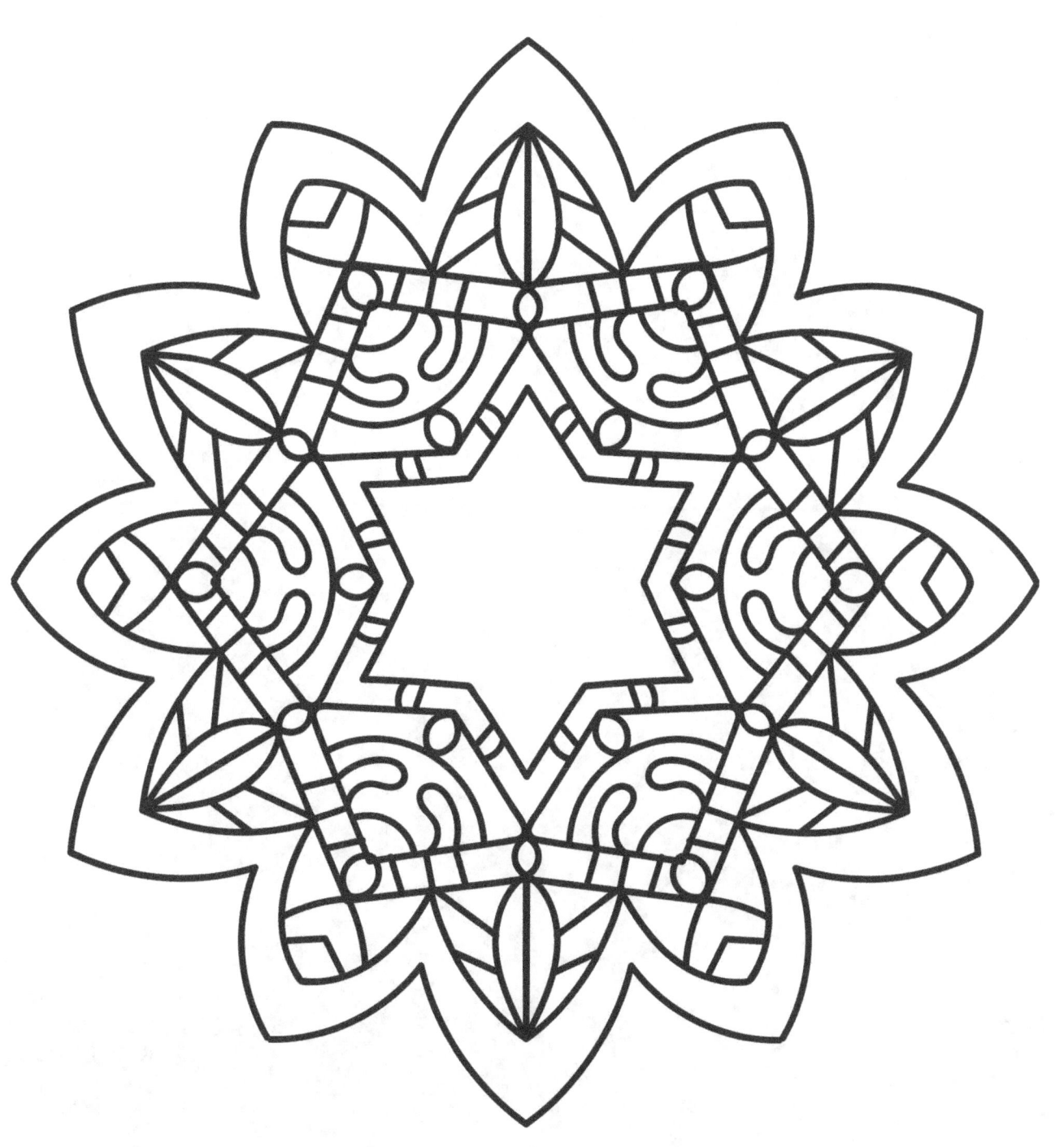

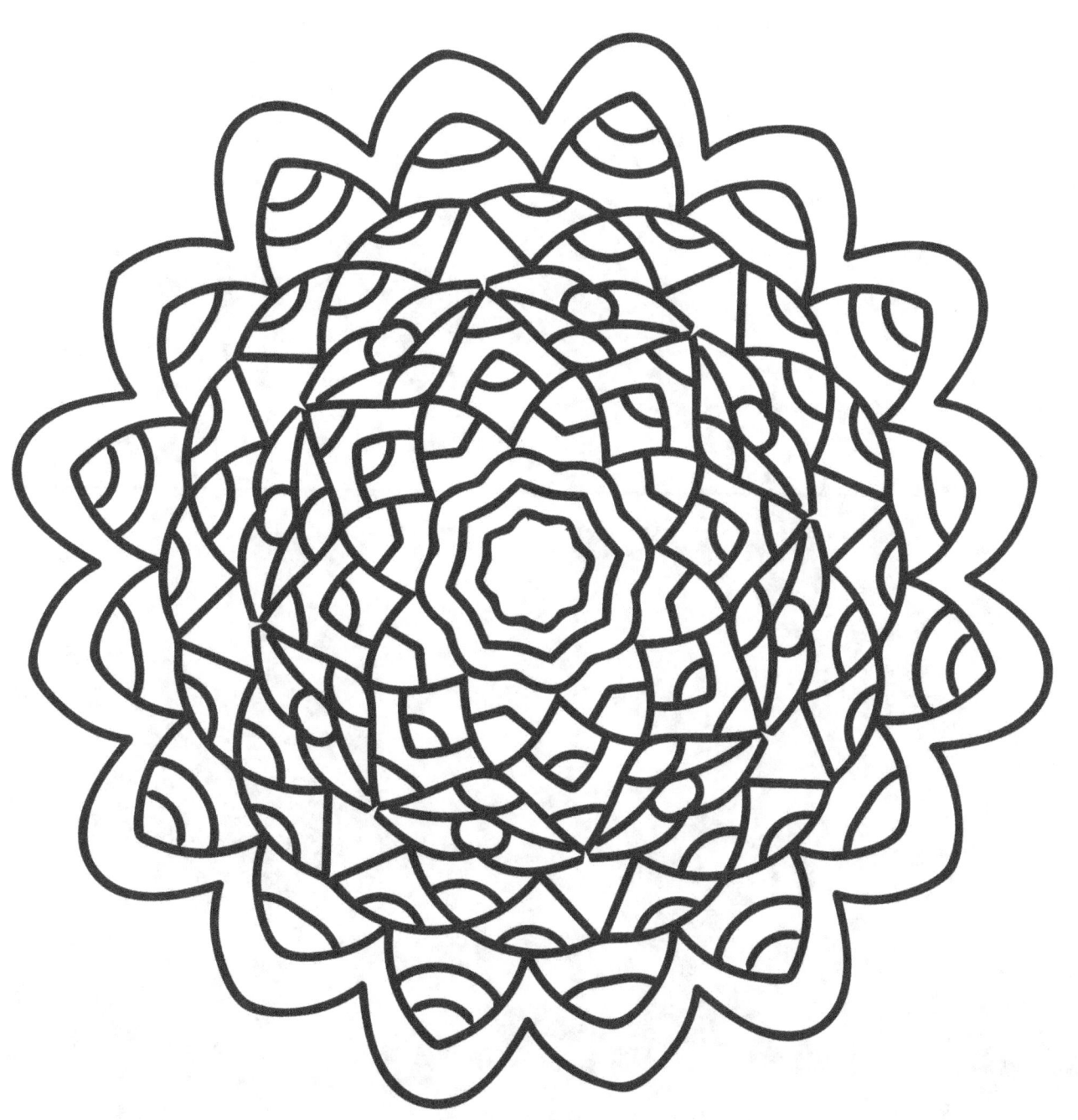

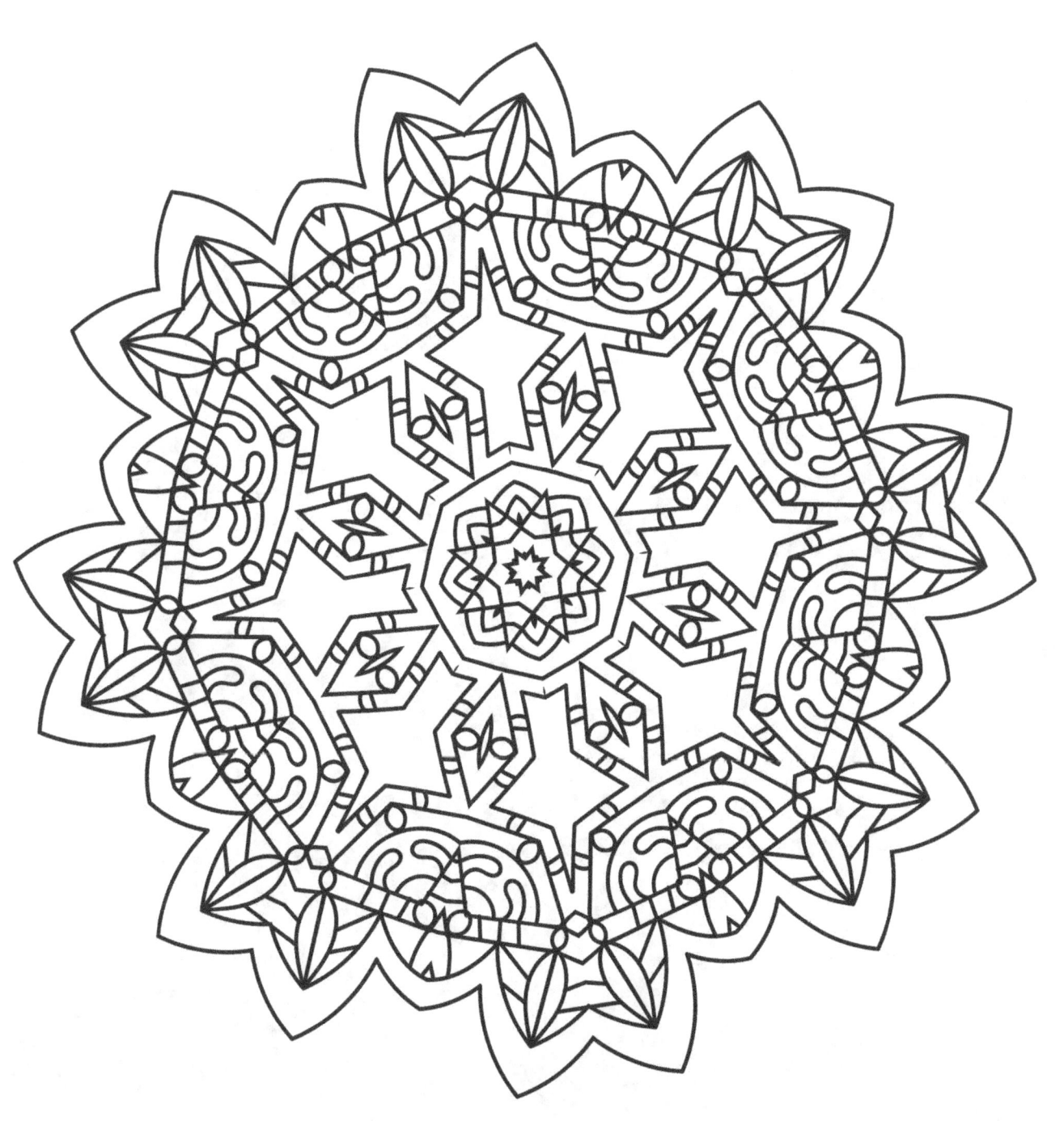

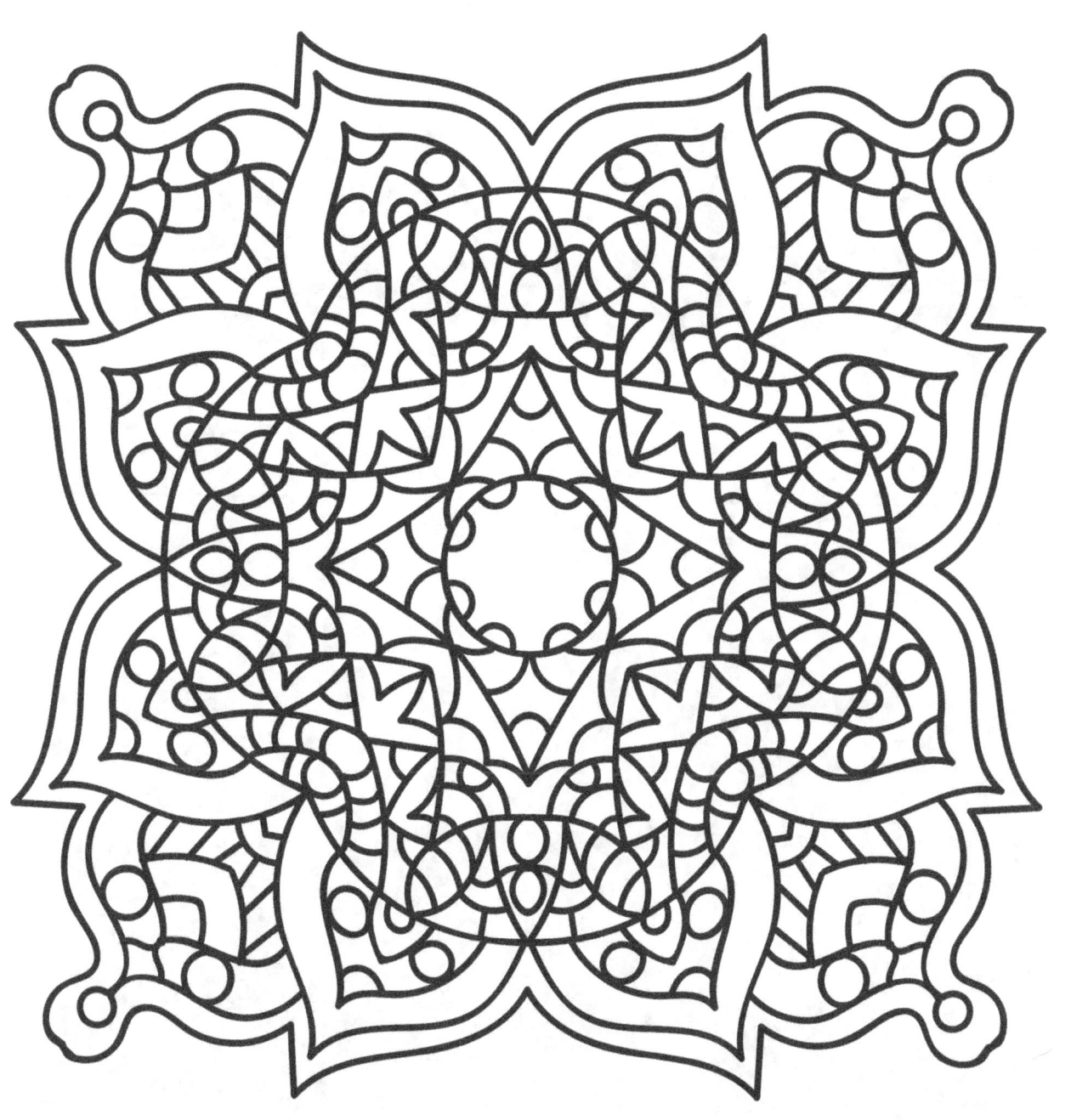

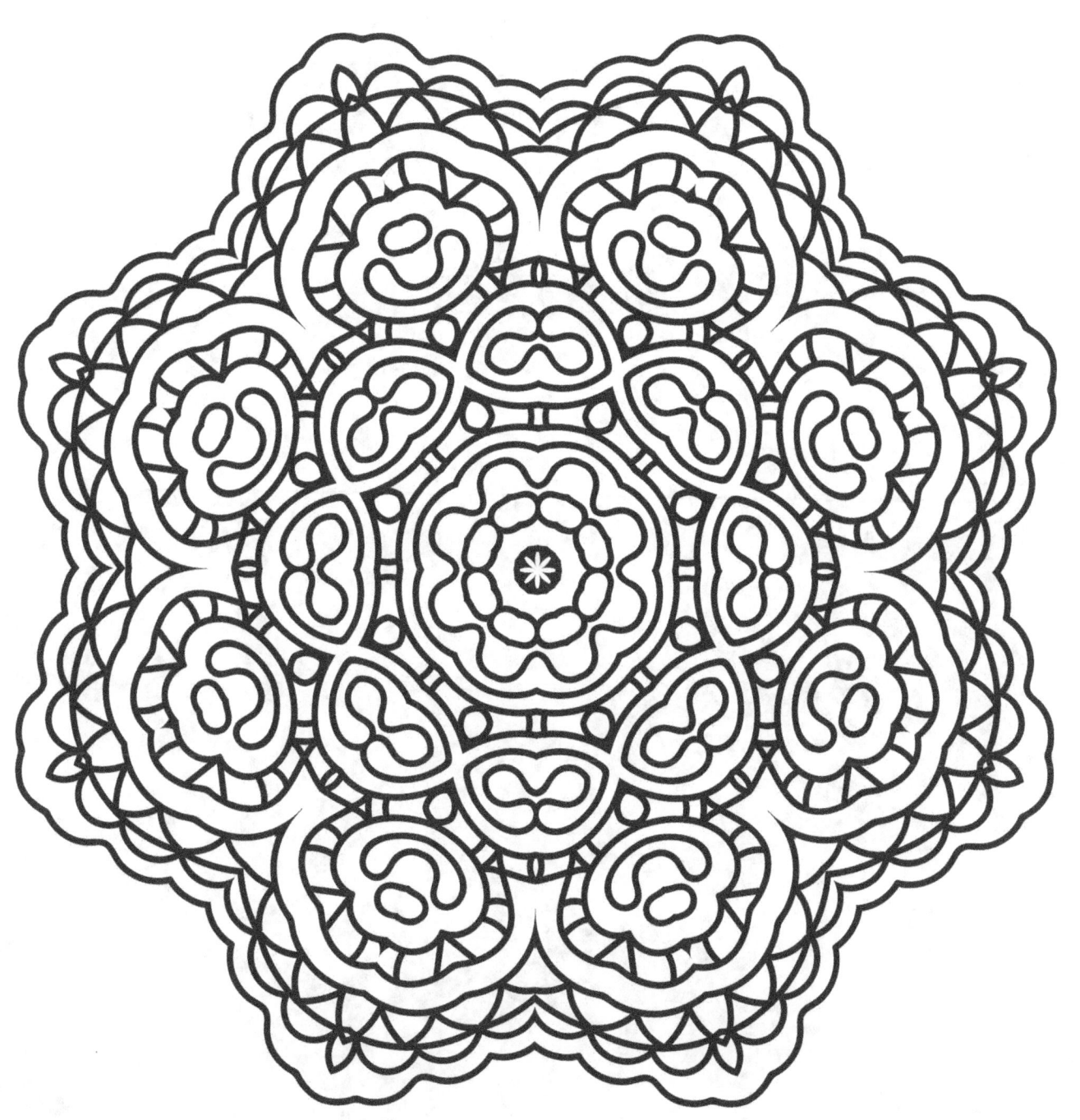

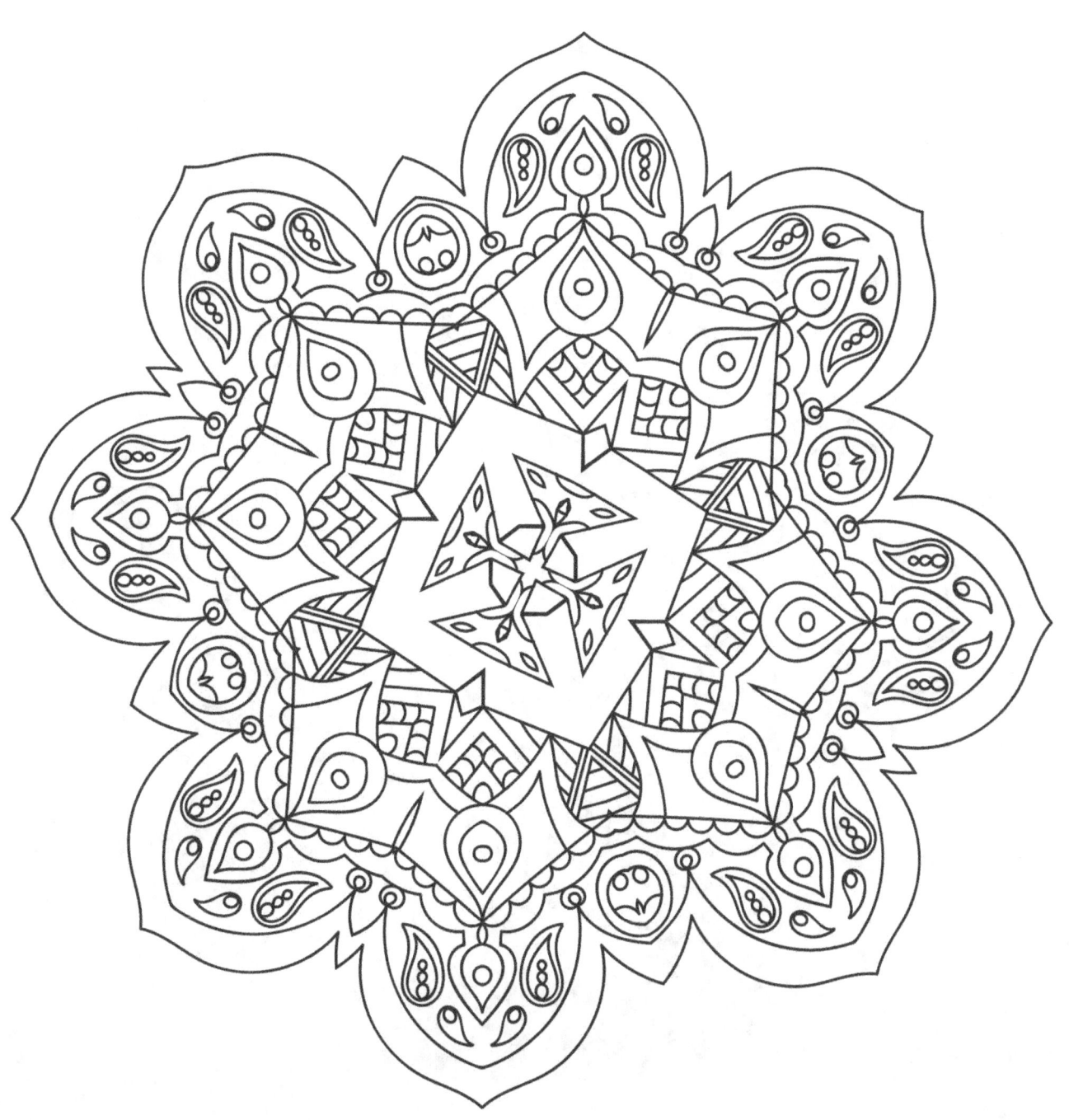

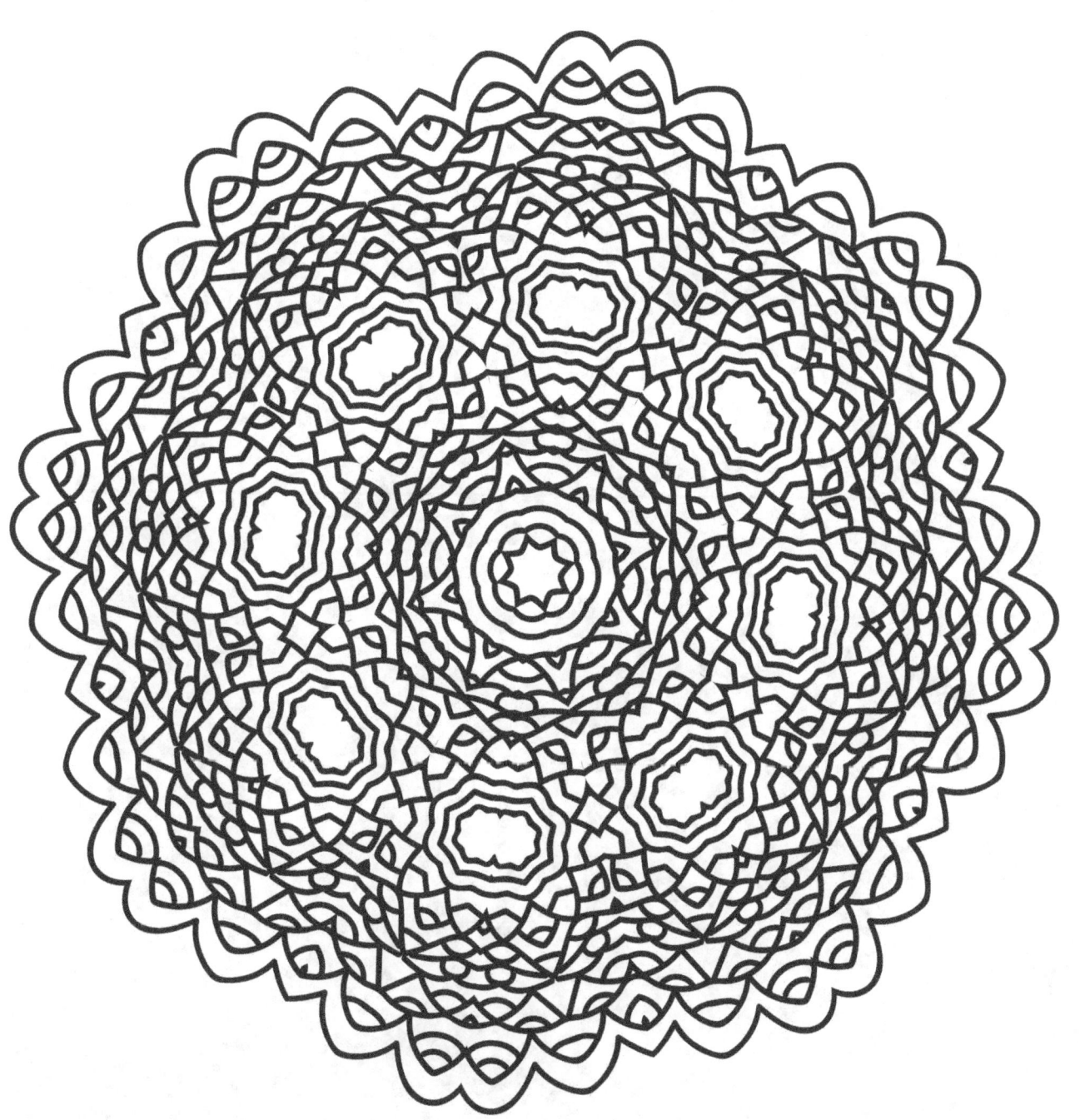

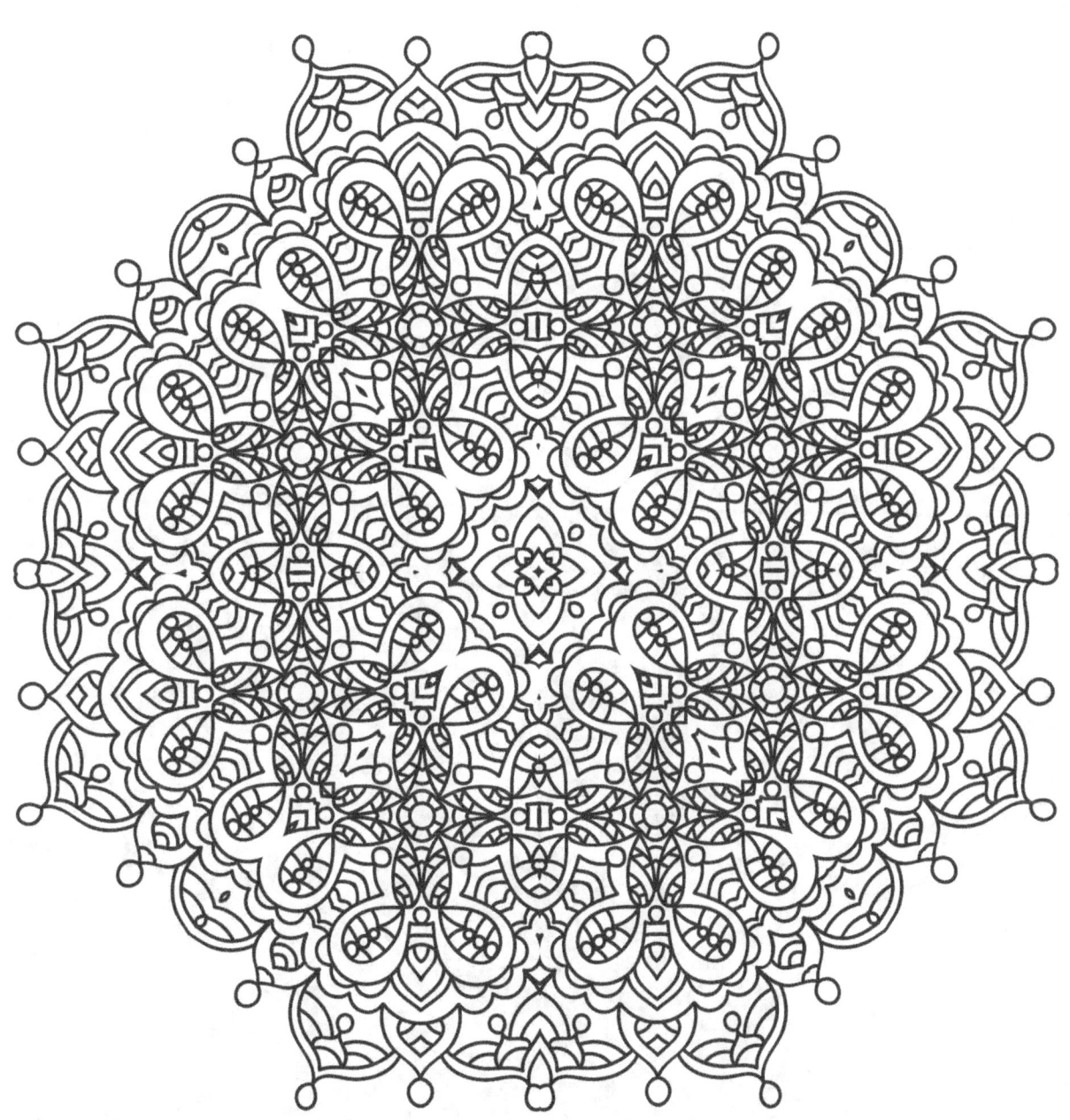

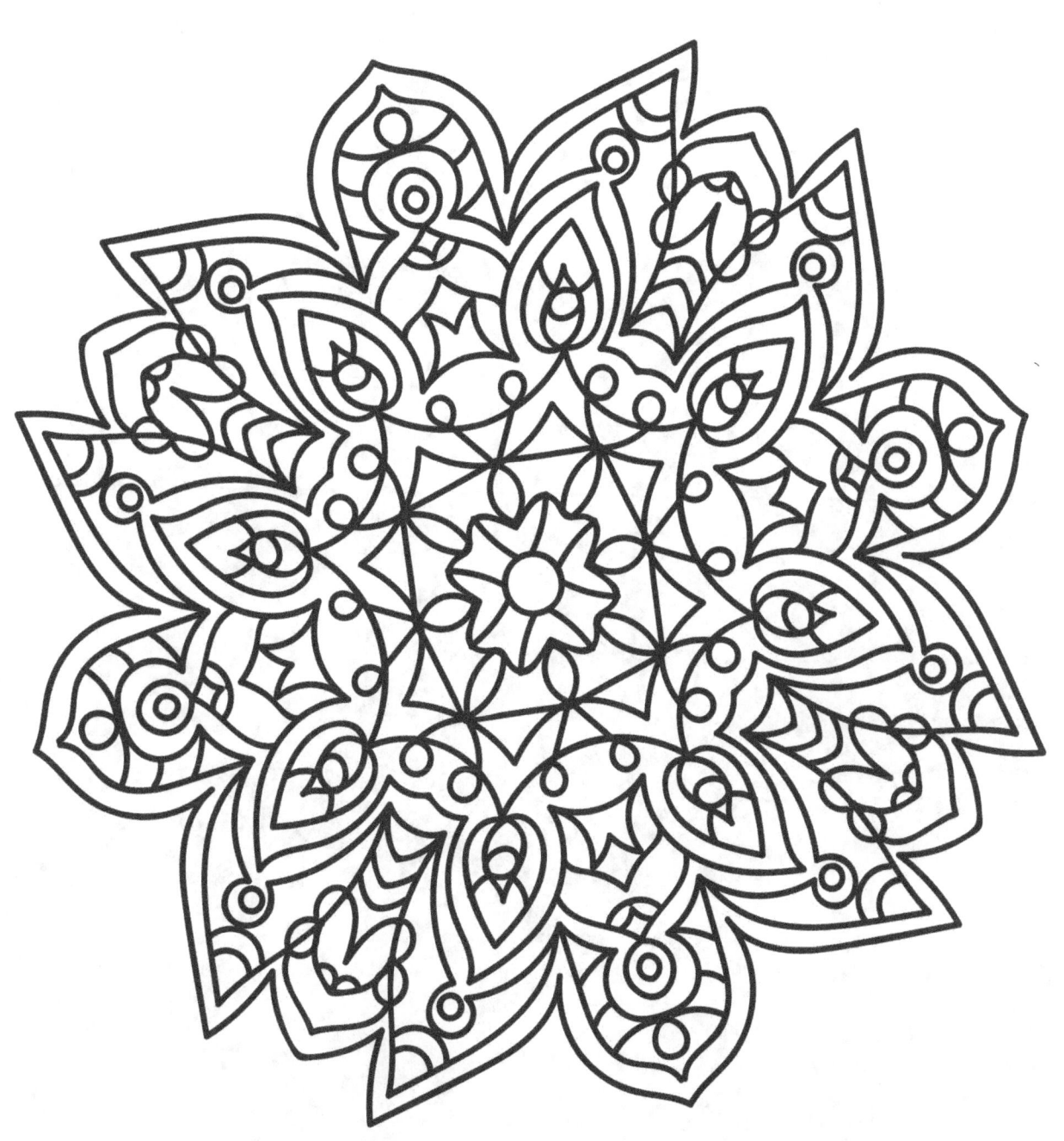

COLOR TEST PAGE

COLOR TEST PAGE

www.ingramcontent.com/pod-product-compliance
Lightning Source LLC
Chambersburg PA
CBHW081629220526
45468CB00009B/2358